To Karen –

With best wishes –

Tom Nichols

2010

Eve of Destruction

Eve of Destruction

The Coming Age of Preventive War

THOMAS M. NICHOLS

PENN

University of Pennsylvania Press

Philadelphia

Published by
University of Pennsylvania Press
Philadelphia, Pennsylvania 19104-4112

Printed in the United States of America on acid-free paper

10 9 8 7 6 5 4 3 2 1

A Cataloging-in-Publication Record is available from the Library of Congress
ISBN-13: 978-0-8122-4066-5
ISBN-10: 0-8122-4066-9

For my daughter, Hope Virginia
with the sincere wish for her future
that every word in the title of this book is wrong.

Contents

Preface

I've never worked on a project as maddening as *Eve of Destruction.*

An obvious question, I suppose, is why I chose to look into the problem of preventive war at all. Initially, some readers of earlier work related to this book thought my interest in changing norms about preventive violence must have been spurred by the publication of the U.S. National Security Strategy in 2002, or perhaps by the invasion of Iraq the following year. To be perfectly honest, however, I didn't much consider the National Security Strategy one way or another when it came out, just as I did not pay much attention to any of its predecessors. I assumed only that the White House was now stating explicitly its interest in what had always been an unspoken option. Likewise, since the flawed end of the first Gulf War in 1991, which I had watched from my position at the time as an aide in the U.S. Senate, I had long assumed that sooner or later the United States and Saddam Hussein's Iraq were going to settle their unfinished business, one way or another.

Rather, throughout the 1990s, I had an uncomfortable sense, like many other observers, that something in the international system was amiss. Even if the great powers had always believed in acting in their own interest, there was always the tacit agreement that they would at least pretend to honor the idea, enshrined in the Peace of Westphalia in 1648, that states should not interfere in the internal affairs of their neighbors. After the end of the Cold War, as a string of interventions took place from Somalia to Kosovo, the Westphalian deal seemed to be coming apart, even if no one was willing to say so outright.

The more immediate catalyst to my research on preventive war was a string of rather alarming statements that were coming out of Moscow in late 2003, in which the Russians (as I discuss in Chapter 4) were explicitly insisting on the right to take preventive military action anywhere in the world they felt their national interests threatened. In an earlier life, I was a Sovietologist, and I still follow events in Russia closely; at first I thought the cascade of threats and warnings from Russian defense and security officials represented perhaps just some of the usual bluster from Moscow I had read many times before. But the more I looked into events in Russia, the more I found that the Russians were giving a great deal of serious thought to issues of prevention and had been for some time.

More intriguing, I also found that the Russians were hardly alone in their interest in using force in the absence of an immediate threat and, if necessary, without so much as a by-your-leave from the United Nations or anyone else. More research produced more surprises, as I found similar attitudes being voiced in France, Australia, Great Britain, Japan, and elsewhere. As in Russia, these were debates that seemed to have been brewing, if quietly, for some years. Discussions with colleagues in Europe were especially eye-opening; when I said I had a suspicion that a global norm of prevention was on the rise, I was congratulated on discovering the obvious.

Yet, I had little success in getting anyone in the United States, Europe, or Asia to discuss preventive war on the record, even among now-retired policy makers, despite the fact that it is obviously the subject of intense debate around the world. I tried to arrange interviews on the subject, for example, in a major Asian capital, but my informal requests were treated as almost impolite, and answered with chilly refusals. I had somewhat better luck in Europe, but in other cases my requests were deflected to lower-level officials or delegated to civilian defense think-tanks. Surprisingly, the Russians were the most forthcoming, and I gladly express my gratitude to the government of the Russian Federation for being very accommodating in my request for interviews at both the foreign and defense ministries. But even Russian officials were, to put it gently, inconsistent in my discussions with them. This is not to say they were disingenuous: my conversations in Russia were among the most enlightening and interesting I had in my travels. Rather, I had the sense that the Russians, like so many other people, were wrestling with foreign policy and national security problems that are fundamentally unprecedented in their experience.

But this difficulty in getting foreign governments or their defense analysts to speak on the record is not why this project was so maddening. I did not expect that any government, including my own, would send a spokesman to jettison three centuries of international law and custom, abjure reliance on the holy grail of deterrence, and openly advocate for the sin of preventive war.

Rather, what I found most frustrating was the degree to which the entire subject of preventive violence has become so polarizing, to the point where reasoned debate, or simply even discussion of the empirical investigation, is almost impossible.

During the writing of this study, I found that reactions to questions about preventive war tended to vary, as is often the case with controversial issues, according to previously held beliefs. On one side, people who would generally consider themselves liberals were literally enraged by even the mention of the subject, and at times I was accused of researching the problem only so that I could serve as an apologist for nefarious neoconservative schemes in Iraq—despite my obvious misgivings about the Iraqi fiasco. (That I teach in a military institution didn't help matters.) Conservatives, by contrast, noted my objections to the potentially untrammeled and unregulated exercise of American power, and I was reproached for apparently trying to hand the beloved sovereignty of the United States of America over to hostile Third World socialists in the United Nations—despite my obvious skepticism about the UN. As for the overarching question of whether we are now living in a new age of prevention, those who think of themselves as unilateralists didn't care, and advocates of multilateralism prayed it wasn't so. But few people, it seemed, wanted the question of the preventive taboo raised explicitly, even though it is obviously on the security agenda of a significant number of nations.

And so I wrote *Eve of Destruction* partly as an empirical investigation into how the world has changed since the end of the Cold War, but also as an attempt to think through the implications of those changes without either carrying the baggage of partisan politics or wandering into the scholastic miasma of increasingly sterile debates between contending schools of international relations theory. (Theory is important. But it should never take on a life of its own, as it so unfortunately has in recent years.) Naturally, the war in Iraq was, as I say in Chapter 5, the elephant in the middle of the room as I undertook this project. But Iraq was not foremost in my mind as I began writing. Rather, I wanted to investigate whether international norms were changing as deeply and rapidly as they seemed to be over the past two decades. The answer, however distressing it may be, became this book.

In the end, people of every political persuasion need to confront the reality that the reassuring predictability of the Cold War—and how odd it is even to write those words—is gone, and that the new and more dangerous world we live in will require solutions that both challenge and offend traditional notions of international organization. Otherwise, the great powers will act as great powers always have, and international order, such that it is, will eventually decay into anarchy. The strongest and most capable nations will rule, but inevitably these powerful states will sooner or later clash over competing claims about threats to their security. Meanwhile, smaller nations will chafe under a tense international peace enforced more by bullets and bombs than by reason and right. Such a truce, the product of coercion and fear rather than cooperation, cannot last, and would only be a short-lived moment on the eve of destruction.

This book faced numerous challenges from conception to completion, and the list of people and institutions who can take credit for its eventual appearance (but not for its flaws, which are mine alone) is lengthy.

Although I had thought about the question of prevention for some time while watching events in Russia, the actual idea of writing about it as a global problem originated with a proposal to the Carnegie Council on Ethics and International Affairs in New York. I was granted a fellowship in the Council's Ethics and Use of Force program, and it was there that I finally was able to conceptualize the question in larger terms about international norms. The Carnegie Council, and its president, Dr. Joel Rosenthal, encouraged me to follow my research wherever it took me, and without the early support of the Council the seeds of this book would never have taken root.

After presenting my findings to the Carnegie Council fellows program, I was encouraged by Nick Rizopoulos to make a presentation at the Carnegie Council Foreign Policy Roundtable. I am grateful both to Nick and to Linda Wrigley (then at *World Policy Journal*) for challenging me to put my initial findings in front of tough but fair-minded audiences who improved the final product and from whom I learned much.

I was also invited to present some of my findings to the Moscow School of Political Studies. I wish to thank the School and its director, Dr. Elena Nemirovskaya, for allowing me to participate in the 2005 seminar in Golitsyno, Russia. I learned a great deal, and had to think very hard about difficult questions that arose in several lively discussions with the future Russian political and business leaders I met there.

Books don't get written by themselves; they require material and institutional support, and I was very fortunate to receive such support from both the Smith Richardson and Naval War College foundations. Without their help this study would not have been written. I owe particular thanks to Nadia Schadlow at Smith Richardson, and to Rear Admiral Joseph Strasser, USN (ret) and Sharyl Jump at the Naval War College Foundation.

I wish to thank as well the Naval War College itself, and especially Rear Admiral Jacob Shuford, USN, president of the College during the writing of this study, and the College provost, Dr. James Giblin, who both have been unfailingly supportive of faculty research and academic freedom in Newport. I hope that this book will help fulfill the Naval War College's mission, as the College's first president, Rear Admiral Stephen Luce, charged us in 1884, to be a place "of original research on all questions relating to war and to statesmanship connected with war, or the prevention of war." Of course, the opinions expressed in this study are mine alone and do not reflect those of any agency of the United States government, nor of the Carnegie Council or of any other organization.

Several colleagues at the War College and at other institutions in the United States, Europe, and Japan provided important assistance, interviews, and insights. I would like to thank Dana Allin, Gilles Andréani, Sergei Baburkin, Robert Cooper, Philippe Errera, General Makhmut Gareev, François Heisbourg, Igor Neverov, General Vladimir Nikishin, Vladimir Ulianov, and Brigadier Peter Williams for their discussions with me, and Andrew Bacevich, Robert Dujarric, Peter Dombrowski, Catherine Kelleher, Robert Lieber, Richard Samuels, John Schindler, and Andrew Wilson for their assistance and comments on various parts of the manuscript. My teaching partner over the past two years, Commander Scott McPherson, USN, has not only endured trying to teach with me during the writing of this book but has been a good friend and colleague throughout. I owe special thanks to Dr. Joan Johnson-Freese of the Naval War College, who was both a steady critic and strong supporter of this project. Even when she disagreed with my conclusions, she believed that there was something important to say about the subject of preventive war, and that I ought to say it. While I know that she does not agree with all the conclusions in this book, I am grateful for her encouragement.

During the writing of this study, I was fortunate to work with several talented research assistants, including Christian Ford, Stephen Elliott, Matt Giardina, and Tyler Moselle (now himself a researcher on human rights issues at the Kennedy School at Harvard). I am also grateful to my students in the "Future of War" classes I taught in 2005 and 2006 at

Harvard University and La Salle University, who brought fresh perspectives to numerous classroom discussions about prevention and preemption.

I also wish to thank the University of Pennsylvania Press, and especially my editor, Bill Finan. Bill's enthusiasm for this project was a great source of encouragement, and I am grateful both to him and to the editors at Penn Press for their support. I would like to thank as well the manuscript's anonymous reviewer at Penn for providing direct and helpful recommendations, which were incorporated into the study.

Finally, I owe a great debt to my wife, Linda. She provided insights and advice on important questions in the study, and her unerring editorial eye was invaluable, as always. And I am, most of all, grateful to her for being a wonderful mom to the little girl who believes, with good reason, that this book is hers.

This book is dedicated to my daughter, Hope Virginia Nichols, who is four years old as of this writing. She is a child of the post-Cold War era, born in Moscow and adopted in America, something that once would have been impossible. She reminded me, every day, that there are things more important than page counts and proofreading. But I was reminded every day as well that she will live in a world of unforeseeable and terrible dangers. It was always my hope that my child would not know the consuming fear of the Cold War and the nuclear devastation it threatened. Now I find myself hoping that she will not have to live in a world where governments wage constant war against shadows and court disaster over imagined conspiracies, no more than I want her to face a future where people have to leap from burning skyscrapers to escape barbarous attacks, where nuclear waste is a weapon, or where missiles filled with any number of poisons could fall on innocent people at any moment. I would like her to be able to visit the world's great cities and not have to wonder if she is in New York or Rome or Moscow or Sydney on the wrong day. I do not want to see her grow up only to find a world either ruled by state violence or abandoned to terror and chaos.

Perhaps I'm naive, but I'm hopeful there's something in between those extremes, more for her sake than for mine.

Chapter 1

A New Age of Prevention

All Members shall refrain in their international relations from the threat or use of force against the territorial integrity or political independence of any state, or in any other manner inconsistent with the Purposes of the United Nations.

—*United Nations Charter, Article 2(4)*

I don't feel I have to wipe everybody out, Tom. Just my enemies.

—*Michael Corleone,* The Godfather Part II

A New Age of Prevention?

The subject of preventive war is a difficult one, not least because it stirs a basic emotion in most people that it is simply wrong. Traditionally, the idea of using force based on a potential rather than actual threat has been viewed in the international community as morally offensive, akin to punishing an innocent person for a crime he or she might commit but has not. Discussing it in any but the most critical way seems almost to justify it, as it smacks of the gangster's lead-pipe approach to solving disputes and curbing the rise of rival dons. But it is a subject that must be explored as we enter a new age of violence and warfare. We live now in a world where many countries openly ponder whether preventive violence would serve their interests, with some (the United States, Russia, and France, among others) flatly defending the right to resort to such measures. It now seems that the norms of the twentieth century are no longer going to govern the states of the twenty-first, and it is time to consider the meaning of that change and what might be done in its wake.

Actually, preventive war is not all that new a problem. Striking at potential foes before they can pose a greater threat is a temptation as old as human conflict itself, even if the idea of doing harm to others based on speculation about their motives was rarely considered either prudent or just. (The great Prussian statesman Otto von Bismarck famously referred to preventive war as "committing suicide for fear of death.") However, it was not until the early nineteenth century that the common-sense presupposition against preventive violence took on the moral force of an international norm that could govern relations between states, due to a largely, and understandably, forgotten incident in American history.

In 1837, British militia in Canada destroyed an American merchant ship, the *Caroline*, that had been aiding anti-British rebels across the Canadian border. The ship was burned and tossed over Niagara Falls; one American was killed during the raid. The consequent dispute between Washington and London produced not only a British apology, but a more formal understanding of the limits of violence in international affairs. As U.S. Secretary of State Daniel Webster would put it some years later, henceforth the resort to violence in self-defense would be judged by whether it was motivated by a necessity that was "instant, overwhelming, and leaving no choice of means, and no moment for deliberation." This famous formulation, the yardstick by which the legitimacy of military action would be measured, became known in international legal usage as the "*Caroline* test."

It is arguable whether Webster's reasoning had much influence over how states acted—and it surely did little to undermine the culture of preventive thinking that helped fuel World War I—but as late as the Nuremberg tribunals of the 1940s, the "*Caroline* test" was reaffirmed by international jurists, almost word for word, as the standard by which states should judge the actions of others.[1] Thus the destruction of an insignificant ship in what one scholar has called a "comic opera affair" in the early nineteenth century nonetheless led to the establishment of a principle of international life that would govern, at least in theory, the use of force for over 250 years, an era in which military action would have to be justified in the clearest terms as an act of legitimate self protection against an opponent whose own actions foreclosed any other options.[2]

Whether we like it or not, that era is now drawing to a close.

It is important to note at the outset that the first part of this book does not make a normative argument about the desirability or morality of the coming of an age of preventive violence. Rather, the intention here is to show that the international system, for better or worse, is already moving toward a more permissive norm regarding prevention; while there are partisans on both sides of this issue who argue both for and against this more permissive norm, those arguments are rapidly being overtaken by events. At this point, the debate must move past the question of *whether* this norm is being breached, or even whether it should be, and instead explore the implications of the reality that it is *already* collapsing, and to consider what might be done to maintain any possibility of international order in a new era of prevention.

Although it is tempting to trace these alarming changes in international norms to one or two incidents—the terrorist attacks of September 2001 chief among them—they are actually the result of the cumulative and corrosive effects of a series of frightening, even sickening, events that have been inexorably altering the way the international community thinks about security over the past two decades. Since the Cold War's end, and particularly in the first few years of the twenty-first century, the world has seen a parade of atrocities: in New York and Washington, of course, murder and destruction on a scale previously unthinkable in peacetime; in London and Madrid, bombings of public transport; in the Middle East, beheadings broadcast on the Internet; in Russia, mass hostage-takings in a hospital, a theater, and even an elementary school (which resulted the deaths of scores of Russian children). But these outrages did not happen in isolation; they followed a period immediately after the Cold War that saw grotesque campaigns of rape, ethnic cleansing, and even genocide in both Europe and Africa. The nuclear clock, once slowed by the Cold War's end, has been set ticking again by the steady (and now successful) march of the North Korean nuclear program, as well as by the clear intention of Iran's mullahs, and perhaps others, to become members of the nuclear club.

The result of all this is that the peoples and leaders of many nations seem to have reached the limit of their ability to tolerate risk in a world of bewildering and terrifying new threats. Political scientist (later U.S. State Department planning chief) Stephen Krasner wrote in 2005 that if a series of nuclear terrorist attacks were to strike three or four cities concurrently in the developed world, "conventional rules of sovereignty would be abandoned overnight," and preventive strikes, including "full-scale preventive wars" without even the pretense of United Nations approval would become accepted practice.[3] The flaw in Krasner's prediction lies only in his timing: much of what he foresees is already taking place. It has not taken a string of nuclear explosions to push many societies to the end of their patience with states and groups that seem to observe no law, custom, or basic human decency, as well as with international institutions that appear impotent at best and obstructionist at worst. If these frustrations deepen, it may well turn out that, in the future, international order will be secured not by laws or institutions or even by "coalitions of the willing," but rather, in the words of a British general, by "coalitions of the exasperated."[4]

If this comes to pass, the international system will return to a condition of anarchy and bloodshed not seen since the collapse of the League of Nations. This danger, its origins, and what might be done about it are the subjects of this book.

Defining Prevention and Preemption

The most maddening problem with debates about preventive violence is that they are too often muddled by imprecise language, particularly confusion between "prevention" and "preemption." This lack of clarity is often intentional. Everyone would prefer to strike "preemptively," while no one wants to be accused of striking "preventively." This is because preemption has the noble connotation of striking before being struck, a nimble response by bold and vigilant leaders in the face of an obvious danger. Prevention, on the other hand, has the more sinister connotation of Machiavellian plotting, of plans drawn in secret against enemies real or, more likely, imagined. There are elements of truth in both of these caricatures, but before proceeding further it is important to clarify just what "prevention" and "preemption" actually mean—or at least used to mean.

Preemption is the easier concept to define, since traditionally it requires concrete evidence of an immediate attack. This could include any number of actions, including the massing of troops, the firming of supply lines, increasingly hostile activity such as reconnaissance across borders, and similar moves indicating impending military action within a very short time, perhaps only days or even hours. Reacting against these preparations in a kind of spoiling attack is still recognized in both law and tradition as a legitimate act of self-defense, much as domestic law would accept the right of an individual to violently stop another person who was about to do harm. As British scholar Lawrence Freedman has put it, preemption is a "desperate strategy employed in the heat of the crisis."[5] It is acceptable because there is no other choice: strike or be struck.

In recent history, the 1967 war between Israel and its neighbors is most often cited as a well-defined case of legitimate preemption, in which the Israelis launched attacks against an Egyptian-led coalition that was in the process of massing an invasion. Indeed, Israeli action was an instance of "anticipatory self-defense" so obvious that, as international legal expert William O'Brien wrote many years ago, it risks being "an extreme case that may seldom be approximated. Not many threatened states would have both the vulnerability of Israel and the high degree of certainty of an imminent attack threatening national existence."[6] Nonetheless, the immediacy of enemy action and the mortal level of threat in the 1967 case continue to define what many scholars would call the "classic" case of legitimate preemption.[7]

Prevention is a far stickier matter, not least because the attacking power has every incentive to claim a more imminent threat than may actually exist, and thus in turn claim the greater legitimacy of preemption. But prevention in its simplest terms means destroying threats before they can actually coalesce, despite the absence of any direct evidence of immediate danger. Another way to think of prevention is to call it *discretionary* violence, in that it is violence undertaken by choice and with deliberation, proactive rather than reactive. (Critics might argue that there is a better phrase to characterize preventive attack: "unprovoked aggression.") This is action necessitated not by an evident threat, but rather by the desire to eliminate even the possibility of a future menace. This is often a choice based on "now-or-never" calculations, in which the attacker comes to believe that a decision to forgo military action in the near term means risking that the target will become too strong to deal with in the future.

A good example can be found in the first great history of war, Thucydides' account of the tragedy of the Peloponnesian War in the fifth century B.C. The Spartan decision to go to war with Athens, although driven by many disputes that had arisen between the two city-states over the years, was nothing less than a preventive war, in which the Spartans decided to destroy the Athenians before Athens became so great a foe that the opportunity would slip away. Thucydides describes the Spartan reasoning in the unmistakable language of preventive war:

The power of the Athenians had advanced so unmistakably and [Sparta's] own alliance was so threatened, that they decided it could no longer be tolerated.

They resolved that every effort was to be made and Athenian strength was, if possible, to be destroyed by the undertaking of this war.[8]

The actual *casus belli* that provided the immediate spark to twenty-seven years of war was a confrontation between Athens and a Spartan ally over a dispute with a third state in a far-off corner of Greece that did not immediately threaten Sparta itself. But despite the reality that there was no direct threat from Athens, the Spartans felt the balance of power turning so rapidly against them that they chose war when they could still fight one—they hoped—on their own terms.

More recent examples can be found during World War II. The Japanese attack on the United States was a preventive war, designed to disable American naval power long enough for Japan to complete and consolidate its empire in the Pacific. The Japanese did not contemplate a long war with the United States, and some Japanese leaders even assumed that the Americans, once they overcame their initial anger, would decline to fight any further. Likewise, Nazi Germany's invasion of neutral Norway in 1940, out of fear that the British would get there first, was later condemned by international jurists as a preventive attack against a target that was not an imminent danger to Germany.

By comparison, had the Soviets decided to strike at the huge Nazi invasion force massed on their border in June 1941, or had the Americans struck the Japanese fleet en route to Pearl Harbor, these would have been preemptive rather than preventive actions. The Japanese, and particularly the Nazis, were almost recklessly cavalier about making clear their intentions to attack and were in the process of mobilizing their forces to do so, and under the traditional understanding of preemption, the targets of their aggression would have been justified in attacking first.

Notions of preventive war did not end with the fall of the Axis. After the war, when the Soviet Union finally developed nuclear weapons, there was a short-lived debate in the United States over whether to wage preventive war against Moscow while the nuclear balance was still in the West's favor. This was not some crackpot idea hatched by paranoid extremists on the anticommunist fringe; its advocates included William Laurence, the top science writer at the *New York Times*, as well as such noted intellectuals as Bertrand Russell, physicist Leo Szilard, and renowned mathematician John von Neumann, who remarked in 1950: "If you say why not bomb them tomorrow, I say why not today? If you say today at 5 o'clock, I say why not one o'clock?"[9] Some within the U.S. Air Force, in particular, were drawn to a preventive solution to the Soviet dilemma: "We're at war, damn it," said General Orvil Anderson, commandant of the U.S. Air War College in 1950. "Give me the order to do it, and I can break up Russia's five A-bomb nests in a week. And when I went up to Christ—I think I could explain to Him that I had saved civilization."[10] Anderson was not alone in his views, but President Harry Truman dismissed him from his post in any case for his public advocacy of the idea.

In the end, the idea of preventive attacks on the Soviet nuclear program was rejected both on the practical grounds of avoiding a major war with the USSR, and because initiating an unprovoked war was culturally unacceptable to American leaders. Secretary of the Navy Francis Matthews, a strong advocate of prevention, inadvertently recognized this problem in 1950 when he said that such a war would make America "the first aggressors for peace," but that America had no choice but to embrace that responsibility.[11] (This time Truman chastised, but did not fire, his wayward preventionist.) This aversion to striking first was evident in Robert Kennedy's objection to bombing Soviet missiles in Cuba in 1962, which he likened to a second Pearl Harbor. The issue arose again little more than a year later, when communist China stood on the threshold of gaining the bomb. The expression that was used when President John Kennedy's advisors were debating whether to destroy communist China's nascent nuclear program is a perfectly evocative description of preventive war itself: the decision to engage in preventive violence is a decision to "strangle the baby in the cradle."[12]

But what, really, is the difference between the acceptable concept of preemption and the previously prohibited policy of prevention? The temptation to smudge the difference between them is understandable, largely because it is difficult to tell exactly when a possible threat to national security has germinated long enough to become a real threat. Along these lines, one U.S. Air Force officer has suggested differentiating between preventive "war" and a preventive "strike," which is a "short-duration military action designed to remove an enemy's capability before it can be used against us," but this, especially from the enemy's view, is probably a distinction without a difference.[13] A related problem is that prevention can, in a way, be a victim of its own success. Preventive war, as foreign policy thinker Michael Mandelbaum has pointed out, "has a self-canceling quality to it. If it is successful it removes the threat that, were it to grow to menacing proportions, would clearly justify military action. It removes, in effect, the evidence that would convince people of the wisdom of waging war."[14]

Traditionally, the difference between preemption and prevention was found in calculations about timing. Preemption responds to "imminent" threats, while prevention strikes at notional or nascent threats. But the word "imminent" presents a thorny definitional problem. While the concept of "imminence" has long been central to the distinction between prevention and preemption, it has also always been mired in debate about when the test of imminence has been met, and in the end the issue often comes down to a matter of subjective perception. Like Justice Potter Stewart's well-known comment about pornography, imminence is hard to define, but most people think they know it when they see it. At the very least, harking back to Webster and the *Caroline*, imminence seems associated with choice: a threat is imminent when the target has no means to avert it other than to attack. There is no time for diplomacy or negotiation, no ability to appeal to third parties for intercession with the aggressor, no opportunity to neutralize the threat through nonviolent measures. In this way, the condition of "imminence" legitimizes preemption and criminalizes prevention by grounding the use of violence in the classical requirement of just war—which is the basis for much of international law and custom on the subject—that war should be a last resort.

Unfortunately, "imminence" has never been a particularly well-defined guide to action except in the very clearest cases of impending aggression. Even now there is a significant debate about whether the term, insofar as it was ever understood in the first place, has lost its relevance in an era in which threats may come from terrorists and rogue states who may not be willing to do us the service of signaling their intentions with the obvious movements of regular, uniformed military units. This anxiety about the increasing difficulty in identifying threats, a problem magnified both by new technologies and new and unpredictable political actors on the international scene, has in turn created growing confusion and disagreement about the legitimate use of force.

From Melos to Baghdad and Beyond

The accelerating erosion of norms against preventive or discretionary violence is especially striking given how strongly the international community only recently professed its adherence to them. Of course, during the Cold War, as historian Melvyn Leffler has pointed out, "preventive action in the Third World was standard [American] operating procedure," an observation easily applicable to the Soviets as well.[15] Still, the presumption against intervention was so powerful that the two strongest nations on earth felt the need to show their respect for it in principle even in those moments when they felt the need to disregard it in practice: both the Soviets and the Americans dressed their actions in veils of legitimacy regarding "fraternal assistance" and "self-defense" when in fact what they were primarily doing was imposing ideological order in their spheres of control.

But even as they crushed rebellions or tamed unruly allies, they never sank—at least publicly—to the moral poverty of the ancient Athenians at the island of Melos during the Peloponnesian War. The Melians were supposedly neutral in the grinding, endless conflict between Athens and Sparta, but the Athenians decided to seize the island anyway as a precaution against any possible support for their enemy. In an infamous declaration, they told the besieged Melians that there was no need to trifle with arguments about justice or right, and that Melos must submit to Athenian rule because it was the nature of things that "the strong do what they can and the weak suffer what they must."[16] By contrast, actions that could just as easily have been dictated by Moscow or Washington were clothed in legal language that ironically honored the strength of the norm against discretionary uses of force even as it was being violated.

The idea that the world is shifting away from these Cold War norms toward a greater acceptance of discretionary uses of force may seem an odd claim given the amount of international fury directed at U.S. President George W. Bush's policies, which are fundamentally preventive in nature, regardless of efforts by the administration to portray them otherwise.[17] The so-called "Bush Doctrine," enunciated in the 2002 and 2006 National Security Strategy of the United States of America, despite its use of the term "preemption," describes a strategy of prevention with such unapologetic candor that some critics have derided it as little more than a barely veiled justification for the creation of an American empire in which any state or actor resisting American hegemony would suffer Washington's wrath. The 2003 American-led invasion of Iraq—the Bush Doctrine in action—served to confirm the worst fears of the administration's critics at home and abroad, as American forces rolled into Baghdad after the expiration of the president's ultimatum that the Iraqi regime, in effect, either surrender or be destroyed. The Americans, it seemed, had arrived at Melos . . . via Baghdad.

President Bush and his advisors have at times claimed that the United States was fighting a preemptive action in Iraq against an imminent threat, a claim that not even the most generous interpretation of those words can support. Even the president himself on the eve of the war rationalized the invasion in preventive rather than preemptive terms, warning that the risks of inaction were too great and that in "one year, or five years, the power of Iraq to inflict harm on all free nations would be multiplied many times over."[18]

Given the stunning embarrassment of finding that there were no nuclear, biological, or chemical weapons stashed away in Saddam Hussein's palaces, and the consequent miring of American forces in the midst of ongoing sectarian violence in Iraq, it would be logical to expect that the Bush administration's distortion of the concept of preemption would serve to delegitimize both preemption and prevention as viable policy choices. And yet, as two American analysts (both opponents of the Bush Doctrine) noted in 2006, despite the morass in Iraq,

A mounting body of evidence suggests that a significant number of states are beginning to embrace the Bush Doctrine's underlying logic of "preemption," which seems a great deal like preventive war, despite their initial hostility to the Bush Doctrine and continuing widespread opposition to the [2003] Iraq war.[19]

This, they find, represents a trend among "numerous states and international organizations . . . to revise long-held international understandings about when force might be used" that is nothing less than "startling."

This is a puzzle that needs explaining. Are other states seizing on the American example out of opportunism, or even just self-defense? This is a central accusation of critics who have charged that, for many reasons, U.S. policies will "invite imitation and emulation, and get it."[20]

To claim, however, that the Americans—or others, for that matter—are leading a change in international norms risks confusing cause and effect. Analyses that trace these developments to U.S. policies after 2001 cannot explain a striking evolution in beliefs about the use of force on the part of several important actors in the international community over the past twenty years, changes that have been spurred more by the rapid decay of international order since the end of the Cold War than by any single state or actor.

First, traditional injunctions against interference in the internal affairs of sovereign nations have been relaxed, a change which has its origins in the humanitarian disasters of the late twentieth century and which long predates the current debate over preventive war. The very concept of the "state system" itself, in which states were assumed to be unitary and rational actors, has been challenged by the emergence of so-called failed states, zones of chaos where international norms, to say nothing of international law, hold little or no sway.

Second, there has been a steep erosion of faith in the concept of deterrence among both ordinary citizens and political elites in the West. This is a problem rooted in an increasing unwillingness to trust the rationality of terrorists, rogue states, or reckless actors who seem to care little for their own safety—and who may even venerate suicide.

Finally, Western policymakers have been haunted by a stark fear that reckless or suicidal actors could gain weapons of mass destruction. The concurrent spread of ballistic missile technology is a particularly deadly part of the proliferation equation. It is instructive to recall that these are no longer exotic technologies: the atomic bomb is now over sixty years old, and the first launch of a satellite took place a half-century ago. The ability of small actors to inflict immense damage on even the greatest of the great powers—and should they be armed with ballistic missiles, to inflict it unavoidably and immediately—has never been greater and has no parallel in modern history.

The September 2001 terrorist attacks against the United States added greater, even frantic, urgency to these fears. With 9/11, mass suicide terror went from being only a notional concern to a fully realized threat, and the now-demonstrated potential of mass suicide terrorism served as a powerful spur to further thinking about preventive violence. But the preconditions for major changes in the international system were in place long before the first plane ever struck the Twin Towers. As John Gaddis has written, al-Qaeda's attack on the United States was only the final blow to traditional understandings and norms regarding the use of force: "The old distinction between preemption and prevention . . . was one of the many casualties of September 11."[21]

Traditional norms prohibiting preventive or discretionary uses of violence are largely gone, or at best, are in their last years, and it is unlikely they will be restored in the forseeable future. Lamenting their passing is understandable but unproductive; the more pressing business now is to consider how we got here and what to do about it.

Overview

The advent of a new age of preventive violence actually required the collapse of not one but two previous norms: one was the presumption, of course, against preventive war itself, but the other is the notion logically prior to that presumption, the inviolability of state sovereignty. The overturning of this latter norm, perhaps one of the most important, if relatively unheralded, changes in international life since the establishment of the Westphalian order over three centuries ago, is discussed in Chapter 2. Chapter 3 considers the changed security environment since the end of the Cold War, focusing particularly on the question of deterrence—and whether anyone believes in it anymore.

Much of the international debate about how to respond to the threats of the twenty-first century might have been more muted, and seemed less urgent, had it not been spurred by both the shock of the 9/11 attacks in 2001 and the American unveiling of a new security strategy in 2002. Chapter 4 examines not only the international reaction to the U.S. National Security Strategy, but also how states and their leaders have reacted overall to the changes in norms and perceived threats discussed in the previous sections. If advocates of preventive war were found only on Pennsylvania Avenue or Downing Street, or if schemes of prevention were only a temporary partisan fascination among particular political circles, there would be far less reason to be concerned about the likelihood that longstanding international norms might be unraveling. But the rise of prevention is a global phenomenon; many members of the international community, great and small, are reaching the conclusion that their interests are no longer being served by previous norms regarding war, and this means that the increasing use of preventive violence is not likely to be a limited or transient problem.

It is, of course, one thing to talk about preventive war, and entirely another actually to launch one. Chapter 5 explores the circumstances surrounding the 2003 invasion of Iraq and its subsequent impact on the legitimacy, and wisdom, of preventive violence. It is possible that the death and chaos in Iraq will emerge as the best argument yet for holding on to whatever is left of the non-intervention norm. But it is also possible, even likely, that large-scale actions like Iraq will be undertaken rarely and with great caution, while smaller acts of violence, including covert operations, interdictions, targeted killings and the like—many of which will involve breaching state borders and will technically constitute acts of war—will be more prevalent in this first generation of the new age of prevention.

But how will such violence be governed, judged, or sanctioned, if at all? Chapter 6 considers various proposals to this end, and discusses possible courses American foreign policy might take in constructing and leading a new international order.

When the Cold War ended, its exhausted participants turned inward, finally freed from the half-century death grip they had held around each others' throats. The Americans elected a center-left president in 1992 whose campaign staff chanted the famous mantra "It's the economy, stupid," while neo-isolationists on the American right thundered about the need to "put the Denver Boot"—the device used to immobilize the cars of parking ticket scofflaws—on Air Force One and keep the president's plane at home.[22] The defeated Soviet regime disbanded itself and the Russian people set about the task of rebuilding their shattered economy and society. Both superpowers withdrew their forces and their material support from areas where they had formerly competed (places, as the former Soviet ambassador to the U.S. later wrote, only historians now can name) and left behind all the tensions, animosities, and conflict that had predated their arrival decades earlier.[23] Claims that had once been made in Washington and Moscow about how utterly critical these far outposts were to Soviet or American national security seem now almost comical in retrospect, but the situations they left in the wake of their mutual retreat were no laughing matter.

As the leaders in some of these now-unsupervised regions took to the business of massacring their own populations, literally hacking hundreds of thousands of them to pieces, the world looked on in confusion and horror. And it began to dawn on many in the international community that being a "state," with all the attendant rights and protections traditionally associated with that word, might require something more than a flag and a name scribbled on a map. Perhaps more important, an idea began to form that human beings have responsibilities to each other that might be even more important than the legal rights of "governments" hardly worthy of the name. How those responsibilities might be fulfilled was less clear, and remains a contentious issue to this very moment.

We turn now to the story of how these changes in beliefs came about, and how they created the possibility of saving thousands of lives, while also opening the door, for better or worse, to the new age of prevention.

Chapter 2

Humanitarian Intervention, Sovereignty, and Prevention

Relations between nations can no longer be founded on respect for sovereignty—they must be founded on respect for human rights.

—Polish Foreign Minister Bronislaw Geremek, 1999

Already, before September 11th the world's view of the justification of military action had been changing . . . . for me, before September 11th, I was already reaching for a different philosophy in international relations from a traditional one that has held sway since the treaty of Westphalia in 1648; namely that a country's internal affairs are for it and you don't interfere unless it threatens you, or breaches a treaty, or triggers an obligation of alliance.

—British Prime Minister Tony Blair, 2004

For all their differences . . . preventive war and humanitarian intervention have some basic similarities, like fraternal twins who may not look or act alike but who share fundamental characteristics.

—Michael Mandelbaum, 2005

"The Arms of Lucifer"

The idea that members of the international community, collectively or individually, could resort to force and violate the borders of another state in the face of a challenge to human life did not originate as a response to terrorists or proliferators after September 2001. Rather, the foundations for the new age of preventive violence can be found in the failures of the international system when faced with the humanitarian disasters of the 1990s.

In international life, just as in the lives of individual human beings, it sometimes takes a horrible shock, a "moment of clarity," to change entrenched beliefs and habits. During the Cold War, the threat of global devastation was an engrossing fear, and this fear helped to dull the impact of the daily tragedies of the twentieth century. Millions died in civil wars, natural disasters, and famines, with these last too often the product of human malevolence rather than recalcitrant rain clouds. But outrage against these disasters was submerged in the greater terror of the possibility of Armageddon. On occasion the common conscience of humanity would be moved by heartbreaking pictures from places like Ethiopia—itself a good case of an engineered famine—but even then, actions would fall short of emotions. Aid would be delivered, often only to rot on the docks and runways where it was left. The occasional benefit rock concert would be held. But in the end, the world would move on and more people would die anyway. Even though the greatest service the international community could have performed for the victims of such cruelty would have been to intervene against the thuggish regimes who were intentionally starving them, the norm of non-intervention held firm, protected not only by veneration of the Westphalian ideal but also by the missiles of the superpowers, neither of whom would allow action against their clients in the Third World.

The images of famine from the late twentieth century quickly became ubiquitous, with endless footage of children so gaunt and tired that they could not even muster the strength to shoo away the flies crawling across their lips. But it would take events far more brutal and disgusting than mere famines to move several of the major powers to reconsider the very foundations of the international system and to abjure the hypocritical worship of absolute sovereignty. The change came when the images no longer were those of the poor and hungry crowding understaffed food distribution stations, but instead became nightmarish panoramas of rivers choked with bodies—or only parts of bodies—and of the dead stacked like burning cordwood while their murderers rejoiced around the pyre. The gore and brutality of ethnic cleansing, and worse, the return of genocide (once thought vanquished, at least in the developed world), stunned even those hardened to the inhumane excesses of the Cold War.

The events of the 1990s would traumatize statesmen, soldiers, and ordinary citizens alike in a way that the violence and suffering of earlier decades had not. In recalling the slaughter of nearly a million people, including 300,000 children, during the genocide in Rwanda in 1994, the United Nations commander on the scene, Canadian general Romeo

Dallaire, was choked with grief: "I think . . . of all those who died an agonizing death from machete wounds inside the hundreds of swelter-ing churches, chapels, and missions where they'd gone to seek God's protection and ended instead in the arms of Lucifer."[1] Dallaire, like those who lived through horrors like Hitler's genocide, Stalin's purges, and Mao's famines, would never be the same after witnessing the appar-ently bottomless depths to which human beings can sink. He eventually retired from the Canadian armed forces as the highest ranking officer in any military ever diagnosed with Post-Traumatic Stress Disorder.

All this is especially tragic given the initial wave of optimism that fol-lowed the implosion of the Soviet Union. The end of the Cold War was supposed to usher in a new era of peace and cooperation, especially since the superpower competition itself was, for many critics, a common enough explanation of the general violence and chaos in regions that had been armed to the teeth as surrogates of Moscow and Washington. But as the Cold War came to an end and the major powers began to pull away from involvement in the affairs of smaller nations, the fragility of the regimes they left behind became painfully evident. Civil war, mass rape, starvation, and genocide soon came to dominate much of the international landscape, and it is no coincidence that there were almost as many humanitarian interventions in the first decade after the end of the Cold War as there were in the previous thirty years before 1991.[2]

The collapse of the Soviet empire, and the consequent American turn away from international engagement, was supposed to mark the end of an era of conflict. Instead, violent and manipulative "leaders" stepped to the fore as the Soviets and Americans stepped back, and began beat-ing the drums of ancient animosities so hateful that the fifty-year compe-tition between communism and democracy soon seemed almost gentlemanly by comparison.

"What Am I Supposed to Tell My Daughter?"

Norms in the international system do not move like tectonic plates, glid-ing about in reaction to impersonal forces. Rather, they change because of shifts in the perceptions of important segments of societies and their leaders. For example, in July 1995, during the sweeping attacks on Mus-lims in Bosnia, *Washington Post* reporter John Pomfret wrote a story about a young Muslim woman who killed herself in despair, with a stark picture of the woman hanging from a tree at the end of a makeshift noose. It was a heartbreaking story, with witnesses recounting that the woman "sobbed by herself until the moment she scaled the tree."[3]

One of the *Post*'s readers that morning was the vice president of the United States, Al Gore, who had been pressing for action against the Serbian sponsors of the militias that were hunting, raping, and killing Muslims. He met with President Bill Clinton's cabinet shortly after the picture of the dead girl appeared in the *Post* and then across the world, and although he admitted that American policy shouldn't be driven by images, something had to be done: Gore told the Clinton cabinet that in the photo that accompanied Pomfret's story, the woman looked around the same age as his daughter. "My twenty-one-year-old daughter asked about that picture. What am I supposed to tell her? Why is this happening and we're not doing anything?"

"My daughter is surprised this is happening," Gore said, pausing for effect. "I am too."[4]

The president and many of his advisors agreed. But it would take four more years before the full weight of Western power, in the form of NATO air strikes against Serbia, would finally arrive with the same anger and frustration expressed by the vice president's daughter that summer morning in 1995. As awful as the crimes of the Bosnia Serbs were, they were only one factor in a process of change in international norms that began to coalesce in the wake of genocide in Rwanda a year earlier, and which finally reached fruition in NATO's strikes on Serbia during the war for Kosovo in 1999.

But the way to Kosovo did not actually begin in Rwanda. That road began in the bedlam of Somalia's capital, Mogadishu, in 1993, when U.S. forces were ambushed by a local warlord and had to fight their way out of the city. Eighteen soldiers would die in the attempt, and their deaths would help pave the way to American inaction during the genocide in Rwanda. The consequent shame then led to a humanitarian war in Serbia, and eventually, to the overturning of the foundations of the Westphalian idea.

Resolution 724 and the Somalia Syndrome

Eastern Europe was not the only place where regimes were falling like rotting trees after 1989. The government of Somalia, a state aligned at various times during the Cold War with both the Soviet Union and the United States, was overthrown in 1991, shortly after the United States distanced itself from the violent and repressive rule of Somali strong-man Mohamed Siad Barre. Once Siad Barre fell, in the words of a for-mer American ambassador to Mogadishu, the United States "turned out the light, closed the door, and forgot about Somalia."[5] Civil war ensued as rival factions, led by their respective warlords, declared themselves in power. The country disintegrated into chaos, and with the food distribu-tion system paralyzed by the war, a severe famine took hold that killed hundreds of thousands within a year or so.

Events in Somalia between 1991 and 1994 had an important impact on international norms in two ways. First, the devastation of the famine was so ghastly that it spurred an historic act at the United Nations: Secur-ity Council Resolution 724, which for the first time authorized the use of force to provide humanitarian aid without the consent of the nation involved. This act showed, in the words of British scholar Nicholas Wheeler, that "humanitarian intervention was securing a new legitimacy . . . that an era might be dawning in which Western governments, freed from the constraints of the cold war, would use their armies to save strangers in places far away from home."[6] Second, the eventual loss of American lives during the operation, especially given the particular political climate in the United States at the time, created a kind of short-lived "Somalia syndrome" that produced an unwillingness to use force for humanitarian means again. Paradoxically, this would help to spur the use of force later; the casualties of Somalia would lead to inaction and disaster in Rwanda, which in turn would help to produce the cru-sade in Kosovo.

America in the early 1990s was not exactly a propitious environment for the confident employment of U.S. combat forces far from home. Bill Clinton took office in January 1993 determined to focus on a domestic agenda. His predecessor, George H. W. Bush, was seen as a steady and experienced hand in foreign affairs, but that did little to impress voters in the midst of a recession. Bush's job approval numbers, once nudging stratospheric 90-plus levels in the wake of victory over Saddam Hussein in the first Gulf War of 1991, later plummeted, not least because of a perception on the part of many Americans that Bush cared more about what was going on in Red Square or on Downing Street than on Main Street. With the entrance of billionaire Ross Perot in the 1992 race as an anti-Bush candidate, Bush lost, but Clinton entered office already weak-ened by having gained only a plurality of the national vote. More trou-blesome was that questions had been raised during the campaign about

Clinton's avoidance of military service, and there were concerns that this, combined with his lack of a strong majority and his relentless focus on domestic issues, would make the new president uncomfortable with the use of military power.[7]

Unfortunately for President Clinton, his predecessor would bequeath him a major military operation whether he wanted one or not. The horrific situation in Somalia by the end of 1992 was all over the world's television screens. Secretary General Boutros Boutros-Ghali told the United Nations Security Council in December 1992 that millions more would die unless the cycle of "extortion and blackmail" was broken; the president of the Security Council at the time, Hungarian ambassador André Erdos, said that "the situation went too far to be tolerated and too far to use the same methods that we have been using so far."[8]

There was a significant obstacle to action, however: there is no specific mechanism in the United Nations Charter for jumping into the middle of a civil war taking place in the skeletal remains of what used to be a state. The Charter was designed to prevent established states from going to war with each other (or, as it has sometimes been described, to prevent World War II from happening twice). In the end, the Security Council chose to act under Article 39 of Chapter VII of the Charter, which empowers the Council to identify and remedy "any threat to the peace, breach of the peace, or act of aggression." This was based on the Security Council's unanimous declaration—again, for the first time in UN history—that human suffering was *itself* a threat to international order, rather than any repercussions, such as refugee movements, of that suffering outside national borders.[9] This was a historic finding, even though it was achieved by hammering the square peg of a humanitarian disaster into the preexisting round hole of an article relating to general threats to the international order. As French defense thinker François Heisbourg has pointed out, the UN Chapter VII determination was "convenient" but not necessarily accurate, which only proved that in the end, if it chooses, the Security Council "can do whatever it really wants to do."[10]

With a UN decision in place, the United States took the lead. In December 1992, with only six weeks to go in his term, President Bush acted under Resolution 724 by sending 25,000 American troops into Mogadishu to break the famine. Initially, the mission was a success, with U.S. soldiers greeted as neutral forces simply trying to supply food to the hungry. Neither Bush nor Clinton envisioned a larger commitment to

Somalia, and both wanted the American presence scaled back as soon as the situation could be stabilized and then handed off to the United Nations. As the Americans and others began to distribute food—or more precisely, to guard the food so that it could be distributed at all—it seemed that the expedition to Mogadishu might have fulfilled its primary purpose, with the city even returning to some semblance of order.

But as U.S. diplomat Walter Clarke was later to recall, for a warlord, "normalcy is the enemy," especially if he is unsure of his true popularity and has lost his ability to make people dependent on him.[11] This seems to have been the reasoning of Somali warlord Mohamed Farah Aidid, who promptly set out to make war on the United Nations and the United States. His intent was to strip away the image of neutrality enjoyed by the both the U.S. and UN, and drag them into a brawl that would return chaos to Mogadishu and reestablish the power of the warlords—himself chief among them.

The story of Aidid's war with the U.S. and UN forces is a grisly one that began with an ambush on Pakistani UN peacekeepers, 24 of whom were killed. Others contest this version of events, saying that U.S. forces had already begun to target Aidid and that the Pakistanis were attacked due to their "provocative" presence in Aidid's territory.[12] Whether the ambush of the Pakistanis was itself a provocation or a reaction to one, their slayings were intentionally brutal, with some of the victims reportedly even skinned alive. Acting on the belief that allowing attacks on UN blue helmets in Somalia to go unanswered would mean placing peacekeepers everywhere at risk as potential targets, the United States took the bait and decided to bring in Aidid and make an example of him. A game of cat and mouse ensued, with U.S. forces referring to Aidid as "Elvis" as they chased elusive "Elvis sightings" around the capital city.[13] Whether it was wise for the Americans to go after Aidid and thus to personalize the conflict is debatable.[14] But the more important point is that by mid-1993, the United States was engaged not in a humanitarian mission, but rather in open hostilities on foreign soil with the most powerful warlord in Somalia. This led to the events of October 3–4, 1993, a day still celebrated by some in Somalia as "The Day of the Rangers."

The infamous "Black Hawk down" incident is a battle that has been recounted in great detail in a widely read book and a popular movie, and the military details need not detain us here at length.[15] Thinking that they were moving in on Aidid's top lieutenants, and perhaps even "Elvis" himself, U.S. Army Rangers were dispatched to downtown

Mogadishu. Aidid's forces downed two Black Hawk helicopters, and over the course of the next 16 hours nearly a hundred U.S. Rangers found themselves effectively trapped for the night in the middle of Mogadishu, with what seemed to be the entire city at war with them. At dawn, with the help of Malaysian and Pakistani forces, they fought their way to an extraction point at a sports stadium. The Rangers had lost 18 men with more than 80 wounded—meaning that almost every man involved in the operation had been a casualty of some kind. One American was captured and put on display on television, while the body of another was dragged through the streets of Mogadishu. On the other side, enemy casualties were appalling, not just because Aidid's forces were poorly trained, but also because they intentionally armed women and children who stood no chance against professional military forces.[16] While Aidid's representatives later claimed some 350 casualties, the Red Cross estimated that the Rangers had killed closer to a thousand people, although the actual Somali death toll will probably never be known.[17]

The events in Somalia shocked Americans, who thought their armed forces had been on a mission of mercy and now turned to their televisions to find an American soldier's corpse being slung through the streets of a faraway city by a cheering mob. As U.S. National War College Professor Kenneth Allard was later to put it,

When the American people tuned in through their media, and they saw these poor, starving kids, and they saw GIs throwing bags of wheat off the backs of C130s, and they sort of tuned back out again. The next time they tuned in to Somalia, they are seeing the dead bodies of our soldiers being dragged down the street, and they ask themselves, "What happened here? What's wrong with this picture?"[18]

The Clinton administration decided quickly to avoid any further losses and bring the remaining U.S. forces out of the Somali chaos. Critics pointed to this as a "cut and run" strategy that emboldened people like Saddam Hussein and Osama bin Laden, both of whom later indeed claimed that the U.S. withdrawal from Somalia had a definite impact on their thinking about American resolve.[19] Supporters of the withdrawal, however, might well have pointed out that Clinton had campaigned on a promise to the American people to avoid entanglements in foreign controversies that did not involve U.S. interests and to concentrate on problems at home, and that he could not be faulted for trying to put a quick end to a military adventure that his predecessor had begun almost literally as he was walking out the White House door.

Either way, the damage was done. The "Somalia syndrome" settled on Washington, with senior policymakers determined to prevent even one more U.S. soldier from getting killed in some intractable conflict in a part of the world most Americans had no idea even existed. Somalia might well have spelled the end of the humanitarian intervention debate, at least in the United States, for quite some time. It was not difficult, particularly in the America of the early 1990s, to get the electorate to turn away from helping people about whom they knew little, especially if the reward for delivering bags of food is a hail of gunfire and the desecration of the bodies of their dead. And in fact the Americans would stick to their guns on this matter—or more accurately, refuse to brandish their guns any further—even as evidence mounted in another part of Africa that something far worse than Somalia was in the offing.

Rwanda: "Somalia Redux"

The worst attempt at genocide since Hitler tried to exterminate the Jews took place in Rwanda in 1994, when anywhere from 800,000 to a million people were killed in just a matter of months, many of them literally hacked to pieces by rabid gangs. The history of the Rwandan genocide is yet another tangled postcolonial tragedy, where the exit of the imperial power freed the local population not only from the oppression of foreigners but also from any constraints on killing each other. It was a situation that most people in the West did not understand or much care about, and probably still do not; even U.S. secretary of state Warren Christopher initially professed little interest in the matter and had to consult an atlas during the crisis so he would know where Rwanda actually was.[20]

The Rwandan horror was a story of ethnic hatred between two groups that most outsiders would not be able to tell apart, and whom some would argue are essentially the same people in any case. Belgian colonial rulers favored the Tutsi minority and regarded them as superior to the more numerous Hutu, but when they left the areas that would become Rwanda and Burundi after independence in 1962, the Hutu majority predictably sought to turn the tables on the Tutsi. In Burundi, the Tutsi managed to hold onto power through their control of the army, while the Hutu in Rwanda took over the government and set about persecuting the Tutsi minority. A Tutsi diaspora spread to neighboring states (primarily Uganda) and a rebel organization, the Rwandan Patriotic Front (RPF), supported attacks against the Hutu government back home and sought to overthrow the government of Rwanda's Hutu president, Juvenal Habyarimana.

In August 1993, Habyarimana and the RPF worked out a peace accord of a sort, but it showed little promise of holding. Less than a year later, with the help of Cyprien Ntaryamira, the Hutu president of Burundi—himself only newly installed as leader of his own country after the Hutu majority finally gained power there—a more durable agreement seemed within reach. The two presidents were en route back to Rwanda on April 6, 1994, after negotiations held earlier in Tanzania. Their plane was blown from the sky on approach to the airport in Kigali, and the killing started.

It is still unclear who shot down Habyarimana's plane, although there was plenty of motive to go around. Hard-line Hutus in Habyarimana's own government who opposed any accommodation with the Tutsi were obvious suspects, as they were the group that immediately seized power in the wake of the shootdown. This was the initial determination of the U.S. State Department, although a report done ten years after the crash by a French magistrate on behalf of the families of the French crew flying the plane fingered rebel leader—and now Rwandan president—Paul Kagame as the culprit, a charge Kagame not only continues to deny but has since turned back on the French, accusing the French government itself of being behind the crash.[21]

Regardless of who killed the two presidents, the Hutu extremists in the Rwandan military immediately took power in the wake of the crash, despite the fact that Prime Minister Agathe Uwilingiyimana, herself a Hutu, was next in the line of succession. Rather than defer to Uwilingiyimana, the Rwandan military hunted her down and killed her and her family within a day as part of a purge of moderate Hutu leaders. Ten Belgian peacekeepers who had been dispatched to protect her were killed as well. Their bodies were mutilated so badly that UN commander Dallaire accidentally counted eleven, rather than ten, bodies in the "heap of mangled and bloody white flesh" stacked like "sacks of potatoes" in the Kigali morgue.[22]

Hutu militias began a methodical extermination of the Tutsi, an operation that showed careful planning right down to the advance identification of Tutsi homes and cars. More moderate Hutu, now identified by the junta as traitors, were not safe either, but still some ninety percent of the victims of the ensuing violence were Tutsi. The relentless campaign of slaughter killed between eight and ten thousand people a day, a rate that surpassed even some of the Nazi death camps—a particularly gruesome realization given that the Nazis used advanced industrial methods of chemical mass murder while many of the Hutu used crude weapons like machetes and clubs. Some of the more efficient mass killing was done by burning the churches and other buildings where terrified Tutsi had gone to seek shelter.

Eventually, Tutsi rebels returning to Rwanda under Kagame's control bested the Hutu military. A government of national unity led by the RPF was sworn in on July 19, little more than one hundred days after the genocide began. The fighting was over, but something like a tenth of the population of Rwanda—a decimation in the exact sense of the word—had by that point already been shot, burned, stabbed, dismembered, or beaten to death.

The mayhem in Rwanda came only six months after the Battle of Mogadishu, and American policymakers didn't even bother to pretend that the Somali fiasco was not uppermost in their minds. One senior U.S. official later told journalist Samantha Power than when news of the Belgian deaths got to Washington, "it was clear that it was Somalia redux. . . . It was a foregone conclusion that the United States wouldn't intervene and that the concept of UN peacekeeping could not be sacrificed again," while in the Pentagon the feeling was that Rwanda had gone from a "Somalia waiting to happen" to a Somalia that was in fact happening.[23] Nor was America alone; the British and other members of the developed world—including the Belgians, whose soldiers were slaughtered in cold blood without firing a shot—wanted nothing more than to wash their hands of the Rwandan mess lest it become another Somalia. In 2002, Australian defense minister Robert Hill blamed the UN paralysis over Rwanda on "the shadow of Somalia, combined with a somewhat debatable political rationale that national sovereignty and non-intervention should reign supreme even in cases of complete anarchy."[24] And in 2004, ten years after the genocide, Lord David Hannay, former British ambassador to the UN, said: "No one will ever understand Rwanda properly if they don't read it through the prism of Somalia. Why did the international community not do something? Because they were traumatized by the collapse of the mission in Somalia."[25]

Meanwhile, Back in Old Europe . . .

In 2003, U.S. Secretary of Defense Donald Rumsfeld cavalierly referred to French and German objections to the impending war in Iraq as merely the voices of "Old Europe."[26] He meant, probably, to evoke old stereotypes of officious European bureaucrats wringing their hands at the League of Nations while rapacious dictators ran about practicing naked aggression. Rumsfeld had chosen easy targets: the French and German positions (along with that of Belgium, a country the *Wall Street Journal* snidely dismissed as France and Germany's "mini-me minion") implied less concern with Iraqi defiance of the United Nations and more with attempts to create a counterweight to the United States.[27] Still, Rumsfeld's comment had to be considered disingenuous given how many Europeans—and not just in France and Germany—opposed the war on a variety of reasonable grounds.[28]

But Rumsfeld's crack, with its implications of European cowardice and pusillanimity, was more than just a cheap shot. It was also inaccurate.

First, as will be seen, Europeans are not as reticent to take up arms as many Americans believe. But more to the point, anyone looking to find a good example of a loathsome "Old Europe" could have looked not to the Western European leaders and protesters Donald Rumsfeld regarded with such scorn in 2003, but rather a bit farther east less than a decade earlier. Despite their behavior during the Iraq crisis, it was unfair to imply that the French and German governments were the heirs of Neville Chamberlain. But it is undeniable that not ten years earlier, all the nations of Europe—and Europe's greatest ally, the United States—were for a time helpless in facing the heirs of Chamberlain's nemesis, Adolf Hitler, in the former Yugoslavia.

The disintegration of Yugoslavia was, for most of the 1990s, an ongoing train wreck that took place at the same time as the collapse of Somalia and the butchery in Rwanda. (The official end of anything that could be thought of as "Yugoslavia" finally came in 2006, when the last of the Yugoslav republics, Montenegro, happily dissolved its union with Serbia.) As in the case of Africa, the complexities of the Yugoslav disaster are not as important as the changes that occurred in the wake of yet more unbridled killing. While the major powers may have been willing to countenance mass murder in Africa—a continent whose problems had come to seem impossible to solve and whose people were not a priority in Western capitals—there was a certain complacency that the kinds of savagery that were endemic to the South were no longer to be seen in the North. In the 1990s, Serbian militias would destroy the smug self-assurance among Europeans and North Americans that such things could not happen in the North Atlantic community's neighborhood.

Yugoslavia collapsed when it was no longer held together either by the fist of the late dictator Tito or by the fear of Soviet invasion. The Serbian component of the former federation, led by virulent Serbian nationalist Slobodan Milosevic, attempted to create a "Greater Serbia" out of the wreckage of the Yugoslav state. This not only meant resisting the claims of independence made by the other former Yugoslav republics, it meant using ethnic Serbs, particularly in neighboring Bosnia, to make war on their governments and populations. The Serbs did not claim to be attempting to exterminate non-Serbian populations in those areas: that would be, of course, genocide. Instead, a new term entered the political lexicon: "ethnic cleansing."[29] What this meant was that the target population was not slated for destruction; rather, they could avoid death simply by going somewhere else. Where that might be was the problem of the displaced minority. But even the less vicious promises of mere "cleansing" were not to be kept.

In July 1995, in the midst of Bosnia's civil war, Muslims fleeing Bosnian Serb forces crowded into so-called "safe havens" under the protection of the United Nations. One of these was the town of Srebrenica, where thousands of Muslim families had gathered. They were being pursued by Bosnian Serb army leader General Ratko Mladic, a man whose extraordinary violence and cruelty was astonishing even by the grisly standards of the Yugoslav chaos. Mladic stood at the head of a Serb-financed army that included tanks and other heavy weapons, and his reaction to the UN and NATO declarations of "safe havens" was swift and predictable. He attacked them.

Even though limited military action to restrain the Bosnian Serb advances had been authorized by the United Nations, NATO launched only desultory sorties against a few Serb positions, and Mladic, fully confident—and rightly so—of his ability to defeat the outnumbered and vulnerable UN peacekeepers, forced the surrender of Srebrenica. His arrogance and boldness were so monumental that he insisted the commander of UN troops, a Dutch colonel, be photographed drinking a toast with him even as Bosnian Serb soldiers overran the town.

What happened next was a ghastly scene from Old Europe indeed, or at least the Europe of a half-century earlier. The Serbs segregated the Muslim males from their families, over seven thousand in total, and murdered them. The women and children were packed off to Tuzla, another "safe haven" (and the area where the young woman in the famous photograph would hang herself). Although this was supposedly only "ethnic cleansing"—again, as though that were some lower-order or more acceptable crime—the destruction of Muslim villages and particularly the vicious campaigns of mass rape against Muslim women made it clear that the Serbs were bent on erasing the Bosnian Muslims, as well as other non-Serbs from Greater Serbia, literally right down to their DNA.[30]

It should be pointed out that at least some observers of the Bosnian war have since claimed that Bosnian leaders actually welcomed the attack on Srebrenica. There is evidence that the Bosnians used Srebrenica and other safe havens not only as platforms for attacks on Serb forces, but also to carry out atrocities against Serbian civilians. Mladic's motivations for attacking, in this view, were a combination of strategic reckoning and sheer revenge, which do not excuse his utter brutality or the mass murder carried out on his orders, but do suggest that the situation was far more complicated than the world's television cameras were able to capture.

The truth about the massacre at Srebrenica may well become clearer in coming years, but the fact remains that it had a tremendous impact at at the time. Srebrenica quickly became a symbol of what happens when civilized nations fail to act to protect the innocent, and the very name of the town , as one writer has put it, is to this day "a conversation-stopper in polite Western circles."[31]

Srebrenica was just one of many disasters during the Yugoslav wars, but the fall of the putative "safe" areas jolted the international community, and even the usually less interested American public took notice. NATO warned that the line had been drawn at Srebrenica, and that the remaining safe areas, including the Bosnian cities of Gorazde, Tuzla, Bihac, and Sarajevo, really *were* safe this time. The Serbs, as before, wasted no time in making clear that they did not recognize any such havens, and began attacks against them, including the shelling of a market in Sarajevo that killed over three dozen people and wounded several dozen more.

The Clinton administration, still in the grip of the Somalia syndrome, began to fear real political consequences both at home and in NATO for its continued inaction. "I'm getting creamed!" Samantha Power reports

Clinton as yelling during a meeting, and the debate among Clinton's officials, although "influenced by an awareness of genocide, was rooted in politics first and foremost."[32] But politicians do things for a multiplicity of reasons, and by late summer the atrocities of the Bosnian Serbs were so manifest, and public outrage in Europe and even more insular America so great, that action had to be taken. The Serb campaigns in Bosnia were so enraging that they served to overcome important partisan differences in the United States; although some Republicans cynically continued to criticize Clinton for his willingness to use force, others in both parties had had enough. Even Clinton's eventual Republican challenger for the White House in the upcoming election, Senator Bob Dole (who had long been advocating for action against the Serbs) vocally supported the president's eventual decision to lead NATO to battle.

This bipartisan consensus may have been good politics, but it was also an understandable reaction to the bestial campaign taking place in the middle of a continent that U.S. soldiers had died defending against a genocidal maniac only fifty years earlier. Operation Deliberate Force, a sustained bombing of Bosnian Serb forces, began at the end of August. By autumn, a peace would be brokered in meetings in Dayton, Ohio, that would, at least technically, end the war in Bosnia.

Operation Deliberate Force was an important step toward loosening previously restrictive norms on the use of violence, and helped to pave the way for more significant action in 1999. Although NATO's raids took place with the permission of the government on whose soil the bombs would fall, it signaled a willingness, at least among Western governments, to use military power as an instrument of humanitarian relief, particularly when their own outraged populations demanded it. Whether the ensuing Dayton accords were wisely negotiated remains an open question, but it is unlikely that the meeting in the Midwest would have taken place without a commitment from the United States and NATO to use force if the West's terms—and perhaps more importantly, its moral standards—were not met.

The Turning Point: Kosovo

Despite the bombing of his allies in Bosnia, Slobodon Milosevic was far from dissuaded from any further notions of ethnic cleansing after 1995. Within a few years of the Dayton agreement, the Serbians began a campaign against ethnic Albanians in their midst, driving them from their homes by the hundreds of thousands, and in some cases carrying out immediate executions. The Serbian region of Kosovo, primarily Albanian and Muslim, was a hotbed of secessionist activity, and the Serbs, spurred by Milosevic's venomous policies, clearly intended to solve the problem of Kosovo's Albanians by making sure there were to be no more Albanians in Kosovo. The UN Security Council passed Resolution 1199 in September 1998—with a cautious China abstaining, but not opposing—which declared the Kosovo crisis a threat to the peace under Chapter VII of the UN Charter. As in Somalia, Chapter VII was once again being stretched to define what would normally be considered an internal matter as a threat to international security.

The Russians, however, were adamant that this could not be interpreted as authorizing force against the Serbs. Embroiled as they were in their own endless war in Chechnya, it is understandable that the Russians would not want to see the internationalization of domestic conflicts. Genocide loomed in Yugoslavia, while a veto on any further action loomed in New York.

A truce brokered the following month quickly fell apart, with the Kosovar militias no more interested in it than the Serbs themselves. This is not surprising: the fact that the Serbs were ethnically cleansing Kosovo does not mean the Kosovars were any better partners for peace. When Kosovo's Albanians returned to their homes after the war, many of them repaid Serb cruelty in equal measure, and the Kosovo Liberation Army itself would later be classified by the U.S. government as a terrorist organization. Still, when Serb forces executed 45 Albanian civilians in a small village in January 1999 in reprisal for the killing of two Serb policemen, world opinion grew even more inflamed, and a last attempt at negotiations took place in France over the next two months. Predictably enough, the talks failed, and it seemed, for a time, increasingly possible that the expulsion of 400,000 Kosovars and the murders of several hundred more could be just the beginning of a genocidal Serb rampage over the coming winter.

By this point, the experiences of the previous five years were finally having a cumulative effect on Western leaders. American Secretary of State Madeleine Albright, Power writes, along with the rest of the Clinton national security team, "remembered Srebrenica, were still coming to grips with guilt over the Rwanda genocide, and were looking to make amends"; moreover, "U.S. officials were [now] accompanied by far more aggressive European diplomats than they had known in the mid-1990s."[33] NATO, despite the misgivings of some of its members, was not going to allow its collective values offended and its collective credibility destroyed by tolerating genocide in the middle of Europe itself.

Operation Allied Force, with contributions from all NATO members (including even Germany, in its first foray into combat since 1945) was launched in March 1999. Thousands of sorties were flown against Serbia itself, for the first time bringing the pain of war directly to the Milosevic regime and the Serbian population. The operation ended in June, when the Yugoslav government agreed to withdraw its military and police forces from Kosovo and to allow the United Nations to police the region.

The launching of NATO's jets against Yugoslavia represented nothing less than the beginning of the end of the Westphalian world order. As Harvard professor Stanley Hoffmann later noted, after Kosovo "a new norm was established: collective intervention against a government committing serious human rights violations could be justified, especially when these violations threaten regional or international peace and security."[34] But the threat to "international peace" in the Yugoslav situation was, as in Somalia, more notional than actual, and what Kosovo really represented was a turning point in which major powers in the international system made clear that they would go to war not only for traditional reasons of state, but to defend moral precepts they valued so highly as to count them as part of their national interest. The war against Yugoslavia, Tony Blair told an audience in Chicago in 1999, was "a just war, based not on any territorial ambitions but on values," and he admitted that twenty years earlier, "we would not have been fighting in Kosovo. We would have turned our backs on it. The fact that we are engaged is the result of a wide range of changes—the end of the Cold War; changing technology; the spread of democracy. But it is bigger than that. I believe the world has changed in a more fundamental way."[35]

There were, and are, forceful critics of this kind of thinking. Conservative columnist Charles Krauthammer, for example, argued at the time that "highfalutin moral principles are impossible guides to foreign policy," and he derided the Kosovo affair, and the putative "Clinton Doctrine" it represented of opposing ethnic violence, as an ill-conceived "blanket anti-son of a bitch policy" that was "soothing, satisfying and empty . . . not a policy at all but righteous self-delusion."[36] Others made more cynical accusations; the Russians, in particular, initially charged that Kosovo represented a crude Western attempt to expand NATO's influence in Central Europe. But a year after the campaign, Nicholas Wheeler succinctly noted that

neither Russia nor other critics have adduced any compelling evidence to support their contention that traditional motives of *realpolitik* explain Operation Allied Force. Instead, the evidence points to this being a case where a key determinant of the use of force was the [British] Prime Minister's and the [American] President's belief that this was a Just War.[37]

Thus the bargain of Westphalia, in which the conduct of a sovereign state's internal matters was no business of any of its neighbors, was finally broken.

After Kosovo: The End of the Old Order

In 1993, historian Marc Trachtenberg, in thinking about whether norms regarding intervention were changing, wrote of a "long-term historical trend"

toward increasing recognition of the right of the civilized world to uphold certain standards of behavior—that states, for example, should not be free to massacre their own citizens or allow their territory to serve as a base for piracy or terrorism. As a political force, this factor was held in suspension by the Cold War, but the ending of that conflict can be expected to free it up.[38]

Only six years later, the United Nations secretary general would confirm Trachtenberg's prediction.

Looking back at Rwanda and Kosovo, Kofi Annan gave a seminal speech to the United Nations in 1999, in which he seemed to realize that the international community had crossed a threshold and taken a step toward a new international order. The "sovereign state," he said, "in its most basic sense, is being redefined by the forces of globalization and international cooperation."

While the genocide in Rwanda will define for our generation the consequences of inaction in the face of mass murder, the more recent conflict in Kosovo has prompted important questions about the consequences of action in the absence of complete unity on the part of the international community.

The inability of the international community in the case of Kosovo to reconcile these two equally compelling interests—universal legitimacy and effectiveness in defense of human rights—can be viewed only as a tragedy. It has revealed the core challenge to the Security Council and to the United Nations as a whole in the next century: to forge unity behind the principle that massive and systematic violations of human rights—wherever they may take place—should not be allowed to stand.[39]

Annan then bowed to new realities by embracing—within carefully defined limits—the idea that states can and perhaps even should interfere in the internal affairs of others: "This developing international norm in favor of intervention to protect civilians from wholesale slaughter will no doubt continue to pose profound challenges to the international community. . . . But it is an evolution we should welcome."

Of course, operations in Kosovo and Annan's subsequent worries about the damage done to the credibility of the UN provoked controversy, particularly in the General Assembly. As legal scholar Michael Glennon noted, Annan's speech

led to weeks of debate among UN members. Of the nations that spoke out in public, roughly a third appeared to favor humanitarian intervention under some circumstances. Another third opposed it across the board, and the remaining third were equivocal or noncommittal. The proponents, it is important to note, were primarily Western democracies. The opponents, meanwhile, were mostly Latin American, African, and Arab states.[40]

Forceful objections, of course, were understandable and even predictable from autocratic states whose rulers no doubt could see themselves in Slobodan Milosevic's shoes. But the fact remains that a coalition of democracies made clear in Kosovo that they were willing to act without the blessing of the UN, and thus by extension without the say-so of authoritarian states led by men no better than the dictator they had just bombed into submission in Yugoslavia.

The larger question in the aftermath of Kosovo was not whether it was legal, but whether it could happen again.

The immediate defense of Operation Allied Force was that it was the exception that proved the rule regarding the importance of multilateralism, international institutions, and the inviolability of national sovereignty. Heisbourg, for example, argued that. regarding Kosovo, the Europeans "tolerated this exception to global multilateralism precisely because it was understood that it was an exception and therefore would not compromise the more general European tendency toward global action."[41] But this analysis was hard to reconcile with the discussions that followed, particularly after Annan's capitulation to the idea that a new norm was in the making. Arguments about "exceptions" were more like wishful thinking, as Glennon charged two years after the war:

Many of those who liked what NATO did [in Kosovo] but are concerned about the action's effect on the [international] legal system simply assert that NATO's action created no precedent. The notion seems to be that *saying* that an act has no precedential effect causes any precedential effect to vanish. (emphasis original)[42]

Even before NATO's air campaign was complete, a new set of norms was emerging, as the international community tried to make sense of the reality of the thousands upon thousands killed and wounded in humanitarian disasters in some of the bloodiest years in global history since World War II.

The translation of "exceptions" into norms became more evident in 2001, when the Canadian government, largely as a response to the controversy following Kosovo and the Annan speech, sponsored the creation of an International Commission on Intervention and State Sovereignty (ICISS). The Commission was composed of a dozen noted political and intellectual figures from several nations. It held symposia around the world, generated a great deal of research, and did a number of interviews during the course of its work. In December 2001, the Commission officially presented its report, *The Responsibility to Protect*, to the UN secretary general. The authors went farther than Annan's mere lamenting of inaction during the disasters of the 1990s, and declared that the international community not only should act to prevent such tragedies, but had a positive *responsibility* to do so.

The commission's co-chair, former Australian foreign minister Gareth Evans, later alluded to the kind of soul-searching that produces such changes in norms and beliefs:

Responding to externally directed aggression, like that of Hitler in 1939 or Saddam Hussein in 1991, has rarely given progressives much trouble. But intervening in civil strife has been much harder for us to embrace. Scarred by Vietnam, we were slow to get it right when confronted through the 1990s with the successive horrors of Somalia, Bosnia, Rwanda and Kosovo. It took us most of that decade to re-learn that war can be a progressive cause: that in some circumstances, threatened genocide conspicuous among them, military intervention is not merely defensible, but a compelling obligation.[43]

Evans also pointed out that the international system was already changing even as the commission was writing its report:

A large and growing gap has been developing between the codified best practice of international behavior as articulated in the UN Charter, whose explicit language emphasizes the respect owed to state sovereignty in its traditional Westphalian sense, and actual state practice as it has evolved in the 56 years since the Charter was signed: the new focus on human rights and, more recently, on human security, emphasizes the *limits* of sovereignty. The Commission was intrigued to find, in its worldwide travels, just how much that gap was acknowledged. (emphasis original)

The commission argued that a "responsibility to protect" is "an emerging international norm, or guiding principle of behavior for the international community of states," and that it could even over time become customary international law.[44]

The Responsibility to Protect made clear that the explicit acceptance of a norm of humanitarian really only reflected the inevitability of the idea, since the existence of such a responsibility was, in fact, a conclusion to which many members of the international system had already come. This was much like what Annan had said two years earlier, but more worrisome for supporters of the United Nations was the degree to which such conclusions reflected frustration with the UN, and this in turn pointed to the sharp question of what states should do if they have a "responsibility" to act but the United Nations deadlocks or is otherwise unable to do so. Evans noted that the ICISS members, for example, affirmed that "to challenge or evade [UN] authority is to undermine a world order based on international law and universal norms"; they also faced the implications of placing the responsibility for intervention with the UN:

But what if the Security Council fails to discharge its own responsibility to protect in a conscience-shocking situation crying out for action, as was the case with Kosovo? A real question arises as to which of two evils is the worse: the damage to international order if the Security Council is bypassed, or the damage to that order if human beings are slaughtered while the Security Council stands by.

The report also drew an obvious conclusion: the repeated inability of the United Nations to act effectively, coupled with successful interventions outside UN auspices, would eventually erode the stature and credibility of the UN and the Security Council. This was in fact what happened after Kosovo, Evans warned, adding that the UN "cannot afford to drop the ball too many times on that scale."

And indeed, for critics of the United Nations, Rwanda and Kosovo still remain a kind of short-hand insult that can be deployed when the UN attempts to assert itself. When Annan declared that a U.S.-led attack against Iraq in 2003 without UN sanction would violate the UN Charter, the American response was to throw the UN's previous paralysis in Annan's face—an especially brassy display given how much U.S. policy itself had contributed to that paralysis—and to charge that failure to support a war against Saddam Hussein would mean that the UN had "failed to act once again" as it had in Rwanda and Kosovo.[45]

The "responsibility to protect" as a principle of international life has since been the source of significant debate, but it is still with us. As Heisbourg has noted, the ability to intervene in humanitarian disasters became so well established that the UN would probably have had stronger grounds to act against the North Korean famine than against Pyongyang's nuclear ambitions.[46] There have been dedicated attempts to limit and even gut some of its major provisions; at the 2005 World Summit at the UN, significant portions of the Summit report on the matter came under attack and the final report was certainly far weaker than what the original ICISS authors might have wanted. Even the United States—supported, ironically enough, by Russia and China—managed to pare down the Security Council's responsibility in such crises from "an obligation to act to a commitment to 'stand ready' to act should the prevailing circumstances permit," while other criteria, such as thresholds of just cause and precautionary principles to be observed in the use of force, "were opposed by the United States, who saw them as overly prescriptive and restrictive, and Russia and China, who saw them as too enabling."[47] And in any case, there is nothing to suggest that humanitarian crises are now automatically candidates for international action. As one observer has pointed out, the complete failure of the international community to stop the ongoing slaughter in the Darfur region of Sudan shows that "'genocide' is not a magic word that triggers intervention."[48]

But the important point in all this haggling is the realization that the debate has now shifted from *whether* states may intervene against each other for moral and humanitarian criteria to *when* and *how* they may do so.

This quiet burial of the Westphalian idea of absolute sovereignty means that all the assumptions and institutions founded upon it are now in transition, especially the United Nations. By the time NATO operations in Kosovo ceased, it was already clear that the UN Charter, and the international legal regime it represents, had been overtaken by the practice of states during the 1990s. American legal scholar Anthony Clark Arend put it most bluntly in 2003: "For all practical purposes, the UN Charter framework is dead," although he warned that the United States should not "proclaim the charter dead, [since] many states would rejoice at the funeral and take advantage of such a lawless regime."[49]

In a similar vein, Glennon in 2001 painted a stark picture of how the world actually works, which he describes as "a geopolitical regime over which the strong preside." This regime, he argues,

bears little resemblance to the formal regime of the [UN] Charter. Its ordering principle is not consent but power. Its rules are made not by students' international law journals but by NATO activation orders and the Pentagon's rules of engagement. Its membership is selective. Its participants are the like-minded states of NATO and other Western democracies . . . [who] by and large trust one another because they share the same values. They support the jaw-jawing of the *de facto* regime because they recognize that when pacific dispute settlement fails, it is they who will have to do the heavy lifting: When international order is threatened, whether by aggression—or, as lately, by genocide—they are the ones to restore it.[50]

As early as 1999, many of the major powers were no longer even engaging in the pretense of defending the traditional international order, and were openly refusing to allow themselves to be tied down in legalistic disputes while cities burned and thousands died. When UK foreign secretary Robin Cook told U.S. secretary of state Albright that some of the lawyers consulted by Her Majesty's Government had concerns about the Kosovo operation, Albright replied tersely, "Get new lawyers."[51] While there may be no firm agreement yet on the exact form new norms of intervention might take or how they might finally be codified, Glennon is right to note that "in the meantime, states will continue to intervene, as NATO did in Kosovo, not where law tells them they may, but where wisdom tells them they should, where power tells them they can, and—perhaps—where justice, as they see it, tells them they must."[52]

It remains to be seen whether the kind of interventions seen in Yugoslavia in 1999 will be as tempting in the future after the travails that followed the invasion of Iraq in 2003. But the normative foundations, and perhaps even the initial legal conditions, for such interventions are now settling into place.[53]

From Intervention to Prevention

A new age of preventive war—that is, one in which preventive violence is no longer expressly forbidden by international law or custom—logically had to be preceded by discarding the norms of absolute sovereignty. This collapse of traditional notions of sovereignty is the link between intervention and prevention, between acting in the midst of disaster and acting in anticipation of disaster. That transition has now taken place. It was spurred by the horrific events of the 1990s: although initially delayed by the military fiasco in Somalia, it began to take shape during the subsequent paralysis over Rwanda, gathered strength during the campaign in Bosnia, and finally reached its inevitable conclusion when NATO, heedless of the objections of the United Nations, rained bombs on Serbia. A more permissive approach to preventive action fundamentally requires the repudiation of the idea that events inside the borders of a sovereign state are irrelevant to the conduct of international relations so long as they do not immediately and obviously threaten other members of the international community.

The Cold War is the object lesson here: for all the fussing the United States did about human rights abuses within the Soviet Union, the Americans implicitly accepted that whatever the Soviets did to their own people was their own business. Attempts to tie Soviet internal affairs to overall relations between the superpowers—such as the U.S. Congress tying trade to the treatment of Jews, or Jimmy Carter's dedication to making human rights a major issue with the Soviet leadership—largely failed, not least because such attempts offended the sensibilities of foreign policy traditionalists, even in the United States. "Mr. Minister," Henry Kissinger once said to Soviet Foreign Minister Andrei Gromyko regarding Soviet objections to some of the human rights demands made in the Helsinki Accords, "why are we quibbling over these forms of words? No matter what goes into the final act, I don't believe the Soviet Union will ever do anything it doesn't want to do."[54] Even a Cold Warrior like Ronald Reagan once famously opined that if the Soviets wanted their "Mickey Mouse system," that was fine by him—so long as they did not try to impose it on others. "And I told Mr. Gromyko," Reagan said during the 1984 presidential debate, "we don't like their system. They don't like ours. And we're not [going to] change their system and they sure better not try to change ours."[55]

This was the Westphalian standard at its apogee, guarded by men and women in missile silos who could, at the orders of their national leaders, enforce a norm of non-intervention and absolute sovereignty by killing millions of the enemy in minutes. Perhaps more important, this norm protected not only the American and Soviet coalitions, but everyone else: to intervene against another state, even if just an insignificant player in the Third World, was to court a greater conflict, and while it sometimes occurred, it was done as part of the hard-nosed calculation of war, cold or otherwise, and not as an expression of national values or beliefs.

During the 1990s, however, a new norm of intervention peeled away the traditional protections of state sovereignty. The step from intervention to prevention is a smaller one than it might seem. It was only logical that, sooner or later, some analysts would reach the conclusion that if sovereignty can violated to *stop* the murder of thousands, it can be violated to *prevent* such terrible disasters as well, including terrorist attacks. French scholars Gilles Andréani and Pierre Hassner note that "we cannot ignore the existence of a fundamental issue: why should the 'responsibility to protect' apply only to overt humanitarian crises?"

Why should it not play a part, given the right circumstances, in the elimination of brutal regimes whose resort to violence over the long term has caused just as much suffering as humanitarian crises or wars? Who regrets the fall of Bokassa, Pol Pot or Idi Amin, all of whom were brought down by interventions which were hardly legal? Humanitarianism, security, promotion of democracy: where do we draw the line?[56]

Lee Feinstein (a Clinton administration State Department official) and Princeton legal scholar Anne-Marie Slaughter go farther, arguing for a "duty to prevent" as a corollary to the "duty to protect." They claim there is nothing "radical" in such a proposal; rather, it "simply extrapolates from recent developments in the law of intervention for humanitarian purposes—an area in which over the course of the 1990s old rules proved counter-productive at best, murderous at worst."[57]

Still, without a Cold War chess game, and the pawns in it that were such tempting targets of intervention, why would the major powers now feel the need to intervene anywhere, short of a massive humanitarian disaster? Even such disasters, as the genocide in Darfur has shown, are not necessarily always enough to move the international community to raise its hand in anger. The increased ability to intervene does mean that intervention should be any more attractive an option; as any lawyer knows, after all, opportunity does not equal motive.

And yet, as will be seen, talk of intervention, preemption, and even outright prevention continues to grow in international debates about national security in the 21st century. Why? Has the perception of threat changed among powerful members of the international community? Are traditional solutions to those threats—such as containment and deterrence—less attractive than they once were? Those questions are the subject of the next chapter.

Chapter 3

The End of Deterrence?

The threat of retaliation may not matter much to a terrorist or a rogue nation, so deterrence may not work for them. They may be madder than MAD.

—*U.S. Secretary of Defense William Perry, 1996*

Instead of a status quo, risk-averse adversary against whom deterrence might work, the United States now has gamblers for enemies, many of whom embrace martyrdom and prefer weapons of mass destruction—weapons that can be easily concealed, delivered covertly, and used without warning— perhaps to compensate for vast U.S. conventional superiority but also because "wanton destruction and the targeting of innocents" has become an end in itself.

—*Lawrence Freedman, 2003*

The Cold War . . . or, the Good Old Days

On Christmas Day 1991, Soviet president Mikhail Gorbachev handed the keys of the Kremlin, along with the codes to the massive Soviet nuclear arsenal, over to pro-Western Russian president Boris Yeltsin. In his Christmas address to the American people, U.S. president George H. W. Bush spoke of "the struggle against communism and the threat it posed to our most precious values," a struggle that "forced all nations to live under the specter of nuclear destruction." Declaring the confrontation now over, Bush spoke of the future with hope: "For our children, we must offer them the guarantee of a peaceful and prosperous future, a future grounded in a world built on strong democratic principles, free from the specter of global conflict."[1]

What a difference a decade makes.

It would have been hard to imagine, on that Christmas night so many years ago, that anyone might ever lament the end of the Cold War. The most dangerous threat to Western security—to say nothing of one of the most dismal episodes in human repression since Nazi Germany—had finally been defeated. The collapse of the Soviet Union, safely destroyed from within like a rotting tenement brought down in the middle of a bustling city, was a triumph not only of Western arms and resolve but also of the aspirations of tens of millions of people in Eastern Europe and Central Asia who took their destiny into their own hands and demanded the right to become citizens of republics rather than subjects of an empire.

That this could happen at all supposedly represented a victory as well by a concept that no one could touch, see, or measure, even when it was assumed to be operating at its peak efficiency: deterrence. Deterrence, the elusive condition of fear that stays even the most eager hand from reaching for the gun, kept the peace, averting a nuclear holocaust long enough for all but the most diehard Soviet loyalists to realize not only that the West could never be overcome militarily or ideologically, but also that their own system was inherently unviable, a foolish experiment that turned out to be both sterile and doomed. There is no need to argue (and it would be a false dichotomy in any case) about whether the West brought down the East, or whether the Soviet system was the source of its own demise. The Soviet system may well have been dying from the moment of its birth, but it need not have fallen when, or the way, it did, and Western leaders can take a great deal of credit for the fact that the final moments of the Soviet Union passed with one man's quiet resignation from his office rather than with the streets of New York and Moscow melting into glass. The more important point is that none of it would have happened had deterrence not kept the keys of Armageddon locked safely away.

Or so the story goes. But with the Cold War, and particularly its darkest and most frightening days, becoming an ever dimmer memory, the concept of deterrence no longer occupies the honored place in statecraft that it once did. Indeed, some thinkers even question whether deterrence ever worked at all, and ascribe the continued existence of humankind to a similarly intangible quality: luck.

A new age of prevention is necessarily one in which states are no longer willing to rely on the passive guarantees of deterrence for their security, and instead choose actively to take matters into their own hands. That seems increasingly the case, at least in the United States.

Richard Betts wrote in 2003, "leaders in Washington have . . . become curiously pessimistic about deterrence and containment, which sustained U.S. strategy through 40 years of Cold War against a far more formidable adversary. Why has Washington lost its faith?"[2] It is a question that could be asked in a good many other world capitals as well.

Is the age of deterrence really over?

Deterrence: Keeper of the Peace, or "Lion Powder"?

What exactly *is* deterrence? The word itself comes from the Latin root also found in the word "terror." During the Cold War, the Soviets, for their part, resorted to two Russian words to get the concept across, one meaning, roughly, "fright," the other connoting "restraint." In its common usage, deterrence represents a situation in which a potential enemy does not engage in aggression because the target has made the price of doing so unacceptably high. This is also the fundamental concept of the criminal justice system in most democracies, where penalties for various crimes are hopefully set high enough that criminals will not risk suffering them.

Because it requires calculations and decisions about risk and cost by human beings, deterrence is unavoidably a psychological phenomenon. There is no automatic mechanism, tangible or otherwise, that triggers an objective condition called "deterrence"; rather, people are deterred when they think they are. The trick is to find the thing an opponent fears, the price that he will not pay, in order to stop whatever action is being contemplated. Consequently, because deterrence takes place as a result of human judgment, classical deterrence theory rests on an assumption of universal rationality. It posits all people as transitively ordering their preferences—that is, their preferences are not random and they can be ranked in order of importance—and making careful calculations about the costs and benefits of their various options. Typically, and not unreasonably, deterrence theorists have usually assumed that survival is at the top of that list of preferences.

Of course, deterrence can fail. Put another way, by definition war is a failure of deterrence. But this is most often explained in the literature on deterrence as the result of various kinds of errors on the part of fallible human beings, rather than as a willful (and thus, also by definition, irrational) disregard for the costs of aggression. Such errors might include miscommunication, a misperception of enemy intent or resolve, poor military or diplomatic intelligence, accidents, or other unforesee-able events. Similarly, deterrence can fail when one or both sides in a crisis for whatever reason come to believe that war is inevitable, and that striking first is the best hope, however slim, for victory. A belief in the superiority of offensive operations, for example, and the subsequent exi-gencies of military planning helped to turn what might have been a tran-sient European crisis in 1914 into the most massive conflagration in human history up until that time, as all the major combatants rushed to mobilize quickly rather than be struck first.[3] Many analysts who studied the Great War later posited that a similar dynamic, characterized by fears of an inevitable first strike, would be the surest way to a possible Soviet-American nuclear exchange, a disaster that could take place even if nei-ther side really wanted war.

Barring this kind of catastrophic miscalculation, however, Cold War deterrence theory assumed that both sides were rational and reasonable: in other words, that both preferred peace to war, that enemy leaders valued their own lives and those of their people, and that meaningful communication was possible. This did not mean that nuclear war was impossible, but rather that it would almost certainly be the product of a decision made under nearly unbearable duress during a severe crisis and not a "bolt from the blue" leveled out of inherent hostility. Perhaps even more important, it reflected faith that the enemy, while dangerous and dedicated, was amenable to reason and negotiation.

Accordingly, deterrence theory posits that the superpowers did not annihilate each other because their leaders valued their lives, those of their citizens, and the achievements of their respective systems more than they valued anything that might be contested between them. This might well have been the foundation of the so-called "long peace" of the Cold War, but in itself it may not tell us all that much about deter-rence. Because of the sheer scale of any potential conflict, the Cold War is really the easiest case when discussing deterrence, in the sense that it is easy to assume that no Soviet or American leader could ever really believe that destroying the entire Northern Hemisphere would be the best way to achieve his nation's goals.

But some critics have since argued that any broader application of deterrence theory is merely a hopeful—or worse, fundamentally unreal-istic—description of how peace is kept between nations. Relying on uni-versal assumptions about deterrence, they argue, is too mechanistic and leads to an undue faith that the power of technology is everywhere and always obvious and understood. There is something to this criticism: consider this definition of deterrence by U.S. Air Force general Eugene Habinger in the late 1990s:

Ultimately, deterrence is a package of capabilities, encompassing not just numbers or weapons, but an assured retaliatory capability provided by a diversified, dispersed, and survivable force with positive command and control and effective intelligence and warning systems.[4]

Habinger also asserted that "every nation has its price when it comes to being deterred," a rather chilling comment that does not take into account how high that price might get for either side in a confrontation.[5] It is not difficult to see where critics might object that this kind of rationalist approach does not take into account what we know from experience about the way real human beings make choices about whether and how to go to war.

Strategist Keith Payne, for example, has charged that classical deterrence thinking "leaves no room for the fact that leaders can hold to distorted, self-serving interpretations of reality, rely on dubious sources of information, be motivated by extreme emotions and goals, and esteem some values more highly than their own lives and positions," to say nothing of the effects of things like drugs or illness.[6] Payne himself is an example of a strategist who is not automatically deterred by the idea of nuclear war; he has long advocated that nuclear weapons can be used and that victory in a major nuclear conflict, even with the Soviet Union, was possible.[7]

This is not the same thing as saying that future opponents will necessarily be madmen. In late 2000, Payne headed a study group which included future members of the early Bush administration national security team, and their report showed less concern with irrationality than with a fear of the unknown:

It should not be assumed that rogue states' leaderships, for example, will be any more or less rational than were Soviet leaders. Their decision-making, nevertheless, may be very difficult to anticipate. There is ample evidence that Washington is much less familiar with the variety of factors that could be significant in rogue leadership decision-making than it was with Soviet decision-making. This lack of familiarity will greatly challenge Washington's capacity to understand a rogue challenger's cost-benefit calculus, and thereby devise deterrence policies likely to succeed.

Perhaps even more disturbing, Payne's group suggested that rogue states, "similarly unfamiliar with Washington, may easily misread U.S. intentions and actions, and thereby reduce the prospects for deterrence"; this unfamiliarity, they argued, has little to do with rationality per se, and more to do with understanding enemies who do not know the rules of the nuclear road the way the Soviets did, thus making the "surprise failure of deterrence . . . more likely."[8] In a similar vein, it could be argued that the Cold War, in its way, socialized and educated the superpowers about nuclear weapons, whereas states that acquire just a few bombs either by purchase or through a crash program might, in the words of one observer, "lose the opportunity to understand the immense consequences of possessing nuclear weapons" and therefore be more difficult both to understand and to deter.[9]

Other writers have pointed out that deterrence "is not necessarily a universal construct," and that some deterrence advocates may even have "misinterpreted the U.S.-Soviet deterrence experience itself," in that the world's survival at times might have been more a matter of good fortune than anything else.[10] "We should consider ourselves lucky," one American analyst wrote in 2006, "to have emerged unscathed from the Cold War and not try to rerun the experiment" with rogue states.[11] The near-misses of the Cold War are few but terrifying. In 1983, for example, NATO conducted an exercise, Able Archer, to test its communications for the release of nuclear weapons during a major conflict. The Soviets, however, started to place units in Eastern Europe on alert, apparently believing a real attack was in the offing. Soviet forces stood down when the Americans ended the exercise shortly thereafter. And more than a few students of the Cold War have wondered what might have happened during the Cuban missile crisis had Robert Kennedy and advocates of a naval blockade had not been present in the room as President John Kennedy's advisors were converging on a decision to bomb Cuba—an act that might well have triggered World War III.

Deterrence, in this more critical view, is nothing more than a useless totem, a word representing a kind of magical thinking that places great faith in the hope that the enemy is much like ourselves, and values the things we value (including life). It is like the "lion powder" that a London cabbie, in an old joke, keeps throwing out of his cab to keep lions away. "But there are no lions in London," the bewildered tourist in the back seat protests. "And a good thing, too," the cabbie replies. "The powder doesn't work."

This debate would be mostly of historical interest to scholars of the Cold War were it not for the fact that deterrence, as a concept and as a policy, is under increasing fire from various quarters. Were this pessimism confined to the United States, it might reflect merely the biases of a particular administration, or perhaps even just a small group within an administration. But doubts about the sturdiness of deterrence are not all that new, nor unique to any particular political party, and they are not limited, as will be seen in the next chapter, to just one or two countries. It is a pessimism that is the result of fears about new threats and new kinds of enemies, and to trace the evolution of thinking about those new threats is to trace as well the decline in faith in deterrence.

Proliferation and the Decline of Deterrence

The future, viewed from the top of what was left of the Berlin Wall in 1989, was a promising one. The threat of a planet-killing war began to recede. There would be no global *Götterdammerung*, no ghastly "Day After." But even then, anxieties about the advent of more unpredictable kinds of conflicts were gathering, with traditional notions of deterrence falling under scrutiny in a world no longer governed by the paradoxical security provided by the Cold War. As John LeCarre's fictional British spy George Smiley mused in the 1991 novel *The Secret Pilgrim*, "We won. Not that the victory matters a damn. And perhaps we didn't win anyway. Perhaps they just lost. Or perhaps, without the bonds of ideological conflict to restrain us any more, our troubles are just beginning."

The collapse of the USSR, and the subsequent withdrawal of the superpowers from active supervision of a system of clients and allies, necessarily meant that the world after 1991 would be characterized by greater unpredictability, including an increased threat of proliferation of weapons of mass destruction (WMD), particularly nuclear arms.[12] Indeed, concern about nuclear weapons in the hands of unstable regimes or unknown terrorist groups was so severe that by the mid-1990s Americans felt they were more in danger of nuclear attack than they were during the Cold War.[13] President Bill Clinton's administration— the first truly post-Cold War American presidency—almost from its first days in office concluded that the spread of WMD represented "the most direct threat to U.S. post-Cold War security interests."[14]

Accordingly, the question of coercive nonproliferation—that is, an active solution to the spread of nuclear arms rather than a passive reliance on deterrence—arose almost before the dust from the Soviet collapse had settled. In 1992, Marc Trachtenberg linked the end of the Westphalian norm of absolute sovereignty to a growing temptation to take action against proliferators rather than trust in their intentions:

The idea that the international community has a right to intervene, albeit in exceptional cases, in the internal affairs of independent states—that sovereignty is in important ways limited by the existence of an international community—has suddenly become widely accepted. In particular, it is now often argued that the world community has a right to prevent countries like Iraq, Libya, and North Korea from developing nuclear capabilities—by force if necessary, many would add.[15]

Almost as if to make Trachtenberg's point, MIT professor John Deutsch (later CIA director under Clinton) argued in 1992 for a policy that would simply state that almost any use of a nuclear weapon by anyone, anywhere, "would be considered a casus belli," and that violators of the Nuclear Non-Proliferation Treaty should face not only sanctions but also "the possibility of multilateral, and in exceptional cases, unilateral military action."[16]

Three years later, foreign policy analyst Michael Mandelbaum made a similar argument.

The rogues—Iraq and North Korea most prominent among them—are openly hostile to the United States and are seeking or have sought nuclear weapons. Thwarting them will require strengthening the restrictions on bomb-related material. . . . But these efforts may not suffice. The prevention of proliferation may ultimately require destroying those states' nuclear programs by force.[17]

Mandelbaum presciently noted that attacking the nuclear programs of hostile states would require the American public to embrace the concept of preventive war, which it has never been asked to do. However, he accepted that a nuclear attack on the U.S. could change all that, and the "next Hiroshima could create in American public opinion a consensus in favor of preventive war to keep the bomb out of the hands of rogue states."[18]

To judge by the initial public support for attacking Iraq in late 2002, the deaths of three thousand people in a single terrorist attack in 2001 may well have been enough for many Americans to qualify as Mandelbaum's "next Hiroshima," despite the lack of any evidence whatsoever that Iraq was involved. But the 2002 debate over going to war in Iraq was hardly the first time the Americans and others in the international community were vexed by the question of whether Saddam Hussein, or anyone else, might become a simply intolerable—and more important, undeterrable—threat to international security. Debates related to, but not directly centered on, preventive war in the name of coercive counterproliferation increased in intensity in the late 1990s, and for good reason.

In 1994, for example, the Clinton administration went through a harrowing crisis with North Korea, whose strange and unpredictable leader Kim Jong Il was clearly determined to create a nuclear bomb, an effort that finally succeeded in 2006. Clinton administration defense official Ashton Carter later recalled his dealings with the North Koreans during the crisis:

> They talk about how they're going to turn Seoul into a sea of fire. They're going to turn Tokyo into a sea of fire. They'll ask you, "Where are you from?" And when you tell them where you're from, they'll say, "Well, we're going to turn that into a sea of fire." They asked [U.S. Secretary of Defense] Bill Perry where he was from. Well, he's from San Francisco, and they [said], "Well, we can turn San Francisco into a sea of fire." They have a level of rhetoric that takes your breath away.
>
> I remember [during the 1994 crisis] we were dealing with North Korea, the intelligence experts would come in, and they would say, "Well, that's a very interesting statement by the North Koreans. It's rather conciliatory." And I'd say, "How can you tell that's conciliatory?" And they would say, in effect, "Well, you know, it doesn't say anything about your mother." In North Korean terms, that's conciliatory.[19]

The confrontation might have led to sanctions and perhaps a military confrontation and even war. Clinton's efforts, however, were actually undermined by the president's own nominal envoy, former president Jimmy Carter, who claimed at the last minute to have struck a deal with Pyongyang. This infuriated the Clinton administration, since Carter's actions in North Korea created a solution that solved nothing and imposed restrictions that the North Koreans had no intention of observing.[20]

Meanwhile, Saddam's continued defiance of UN arms inspectors raised fears that he had reconstituted his WMD programs despite the major bombing of Iraqi WMD sites in 1991 and years of subsequent sanctions. Trouble seemed to loom with the Iranians over their nuclear program and their expanding grasp of ballistic missile technology, and even with Libya, which did not abjure the pursuit of nuclear weapons until 2004. Little wonder that in 1996, only two years after the Korean crisis, defense secretary Perry expressed concern about "a future threat that a rogue state, *that may be impossible to deter,* will obtain ICBMs that can reach the United States" (emphasis added).[21]

The question of what to do when faced with a putatively undeterrable opponent generated its own obvious answer in short order. In January 1998, a group of American conservatives, including some who would go on to serve in the Bush administration, such as Donald Rumsfeld and Paul Wolfowitz, sent an open letter to President Clinton, arguing that the "only acceptable strategy is one that eliminates the possibility that Iraq will be able to use or threaten to use weapons of mass destruction," and that "in the long term, it means removing Saddam Hussein and his regime from power."[22] To some extent, the advocacy of a military solution was not surprising given the signatories of the letter, but it was nonetheless remarkable that so many former officials of the United States government would explicitly call for removing the head of a sovereign state.

Bill Clinton, for his part, apparently needed little convincing, as his administration had already begun to lay out the case for a preventive war. In a forceful February 1998 speech at the Pentagon, Clinton made the assertion that not acting against Saddam was tantamount to allowing him to gain, and therefore to use, weapons of mass destruction:

Now, let's imagine the future. What if he fails to comply, and we fail to act, or we take some ambiguous third route which gives him yet more opportunities to develop this program of weapons of mass destruction and continue to press for the release of the sanctions and continue to ignore the solemn commitments that he made? Well, he will conclude that the international community has lost its will. He will then conclude that he can go right on and do more to rebuild an arsenal of devastating destruction. *And some day, some way, I guarantee you, he'll use the arsenal.* And I think every one of you who's really worked on this for any length of time believes that, too. (emphasis added)[23]

By year's end, Clinton made good on his threat to attack Iraq, with U.S. and British forces engaging in a three-day bombing campaign, Operation Desert Fox, aimed at "degrading" Saddam Hussein's presumed WMD capabilities. "Other countries possess weapons of mass destruction and ballistic missiles," Clinton said as the bombing started. "With Saddam, there is one big difference: He has used them . . . and I have no doubt today, that left unchecked, Saddam Hussein will use these terrible weapons again."[24]

For a variety of reasons, including Clinton's domestic political troubles and a face-saving deal struck at in the United Nations, military operations in 1998 never rose to the level of the rhetoric that attended them. Only weeks before Desert Fox, the U.S. Congress passed, and Clinton signed, the 1998 Iraq Liberation Act, which made it the stated policy of the American government from that point onward that Hussein's regime should be removed from power. This was not a party-line vote; the Act passed by a lopsided and bipartisan 360 to 38 vote in the House, and by unanimous consent in the Senate. The Act, however, only "supported" such efforts by the Iraqi opposition and was notably silent on the question of the use of American force. Regime change was never the stated goal of Desert Fox, and in the end the whole thing was a kind of desultory affair whose impact on Iraqi WMD programs remains unclear to this day.[25]

But what is most interesting about this 1998 almost-war against Iraq is the way Clinton and others implicitly argued that opponents like Saddam Hussein were effectively undeterrable. This kind of anxiety could be seen, for example, among Clinton's senior advisors in mid-1998 as they debated whether to strike a Sudanese factory they suspected was making chemical weapons. Former National Security Council staff members Daniel Benjamin and Steven Simon later recalled:

Within the small circle of officials who knew of the plan [to attack the Sudanese facility called al-Shifa], some felt uneasy. Attorney General Janet Reno expressed concern about whether the strikes were proportional and met the requirements of self-defense under Article 51 of the UN Charter, which was how the administration intended to justify them. Others were aware that a decision to attack another country is rarely made on the basis of clandestine intelligence, and the United States has not often pursued a strategy of preempting threats militarily. Yet the perception of imminent danger was powerful enough to overcome these concerns. At the Principals meeting, [National Security Advisor] Sandy Berger asked, "What if we do not hit it and then, after an attack, nerve gas is released in the New York City subway? What will we say then?"

Reno eventually declined to vote, "but the rest recommended unanimously that al-Shifa be destroyed."[26] In August 1998, the United States launched Operation Infinite Reach, a series of cruise missile attacks against the Sudanese facility as well as several al-Qaeda training camps in Afghanistan.

The fact that al-Qaeda was struck was important. Osama bin Laden and his lieutenants were actually the primary targets of Infinite Reach, largely as retaliation for al-Qaeda's involvement in terrorist bombings against U.S. embassies in Africa. But in justifying the operation, Clinton administration officials argued that they were acting against a triple threat, a synergy between Sudan's manufacture of chemical weapons, the Iraqis, and al-Qaeda terrorists. "We see evidence that we think is quite clear on contacts between Sudan and Iraq," undersecretary of state Thomas Pickering said. "In fact, El Shifa [sic] officials, early in the company's history, we believe were in touch with Iraqi individuals associated with Iraq's VX [nerve gas] program."[27] UN ambassador Bill Richardson told CNN's Wolf Blitzer shortly after the strikes:

We know for a fact, physical evidence, soil samples of VX precursor—chemical precursor at the site. Secondly, Wolf, direct evidence of ties between Osama bin Laden and the [Sudanese] Military Industrial Corporation—the al Shifa factory was part of that. This is an operation—a collection of buildings that does a lot of this dirty munitions stuff. And, thirdly, there is no evidence that this precursor has a commercial application. So, you combine that with Sudan support for terrorism, their connections with Iraq on VX, and you combine that, also, with the chemical precursor issue, and Sudan's leadership support for Osama bin Laden, and you've got a pretty clear cut case.[28]

The case, as it turns out, wasn't quite so clear cut, and over the years various investigations have cast doubt on whether the Clinton administration's intelligence on al-Shifa was correct. But all major figures in the execution of Operation Infinite Reach stand by their decision, most notably former defense secretary William Cohen, who repeated the charges against the Sudanese in his 2004 testimony to the 9/11 Commission.[29]

After 9/11, this kind of unwillingness to trust in either diplomacy or deterrence became more widespread, particularly with regard to terrorist organizations. Former U.S. defense official Elaine Bunn wrote in 2003 that "some analysts have come to a working assumption that 'deterring terrorists' is an oxymoron and that in the case of terrorists and WMD, possession equals use"—which is exactly the case Clinton was making about Saddam Hussein five years earlier.[30] Traditional foreign policy realists would later counter these fears about the declining utility of deterrence by arguing, as they always had, that the fundamentals of deterrence were universal, and even applied to the likes of Saddam Hussein.[31] These arguments, obviously, did not win the day in the eventual debate over invading Iraq. By 2003, the experiences of the previous decade had tarnished the word "deterrence" itself; what would have been accepted as given—that states like North Korea and Iraq are deterrable—had become contestable and even dubious in the eyes of key policymakers in the United States and elsewhere.[32]

In the late 1990s, however, there was little in all this of a systematic examination of the question of preventive war. Operation Infinite Reach, at least where the attack on Sudan is concerned, was a preventive strike, but it was phrased in terms of self-defense and preemption. Most concerns instead centered specifically on the intransigence of the North Koreans and especially on the nagging problem of Saddam Hussein. In the 1998 crisis with Iraq, none of the participants squarely confronted the fact that removing Saddam would constitute a preventive war. A few commentators, such as British scholar Marc Weller, did try to warn at the time that Desert Fox and other operations against Iraq "fundamentally challenge the presently existing structures of international order, rather than strengthening them. . . . The unilateral use of force is deemed once more acceptable for purposes other than resisting an armed attack or protecting a population in danger of extermination."[33] But had war against Iraq taken place in 1998, it would have been rationalized both as a matter of self-defense and in the name of enforcing UN mandates, and not in terms of removing a direct threat to the U.S. or its allies, which would have allowed the major belligerents to avoid the question of whether they were collectively repudiating previous norms about the recourse to war. That more thorough examination of the question of preventive action would have to wait until after the worst attack on American soil in history.

The Impact of 9/11

Although the erosion of the traditional prohibition on intervention in the affairs of sovereign states in the 1990s took place at the same that awareness was growing of the problems of terrorism and proliferation, there was little movement in the international community at the time toward a synthesis of these two trends. Terrorism was viewed, at least in the United States, as largely a police matter rather than an international security issue, as former U.S. secretary of state George Schultz later admitted:

In those days [the 1980s] we focused on how to defend against terrorism. We reinforced our embassies and increased our intelligence effort. We thought we made some progress. We established the legal basis for holding states responsible for using terrorists to attack Americans anywhere. Through intelligence, we did abort many potential terrorist acts. But we didn't really understand what motivated the terrorists or what they were out to do.[34]

In part, this was because the non-state nature of terrorist organizations did not fit into the state-centric image of the world held by policymakers, whose formative experiences had been forged by the Cold War and who by habit and training viewed international security problems as issues negotiated between nation-states and established governments.

Terrorism, by contrast, was viewed as a criminal act perpetrated by individuals, and therefore a matter for domestic law enforcement agencies. The U.S. defense and intelligence communities continually resisted seeing anti-terrorist efforts as tantamount to war. One account later noted:

Even after bin Laden declared war on America in a 1998 *fatwa*, and bombed U.S. embassies to show his followers that he meant business in exhorting them to "abide by Allah's order by killing Americans . . . anywhere, anytime, and wherever possible," the Pentagon still resisted calling terrorism war. It wasn't alone. A CIA assessment of the *fatwa* acknowledged that if a *government* had issued such a decree, one would have had to consider it a declaration of war, but in al Qaeda's case it was only propaganda. (emphasis original)[35]

Although there was clearly an awareness of transnational terrorist networks, the elements within them did not represent a coherent enough actor to qualify as a unitary "enemy" in the way a nation-state might, or at least in any way that national security bureaucracies could grasp, particularly in the United States.

This distinction between terrorism and war was shattered with the attacks on New York and Washington in 2001. The response at the highest levels of the American government was immediate: terrorism changed, in the space of minutes, from a law enforcement problem to a dire issue of war and peace. President Bush later recalled his first thought at the very moment he was told the news of the World Trade Center attack: "They had declared war on us, and I made up my mind at that moment that we were going to war."[36] Taking the president's lead, CIA Director George Tenet composed a message to his top leaders at the Agency that began: "We're at War."[37]

America's major allies would not go quite so far, but they, too, immediately reacted as though a major attack had been launched not just at the United States, but at the entire West. What that meant in terms of action, however, was initially unclear. One NATO official later recalled: "There was little to guide us. There had been hardly any discussion of terrorism at NATO up to that point," and there was even some discussion about whether the use of airplanes as weapons constituted an "armed" attack.[38] Resolve and anger displaced such questions (airplanes used as missiles, it was quickly decided, did indeed represent an "armed" attack), and at a meeting the day after New York and Washington were struck, NATO representatives gathered in Brussels and unanimously invoked Article Five of the Atlantic Charter, which declared the attack on the United States to be an attack on all NATO members. On September 14, Australia likewise declared that the ANZUS treaty was being invoked for the first time in its history.

As former Spanish prime minister José María Aznar was later to write, this was a step toward war but also into unknown territory:

September 11 was . . . a strategic revolution for NATO. Traditional concepts like containment and deterrence were no longer viable in the face of global jihadism; relying on passive or reactive defense, as NATO did for more than four decades, meant, in fact, putting at risk the lives of our citizens. Yet going on the offensive, or taking preventive measures against Islamist terror, was something NATO was not prepared to deal with even after activating its collective defense provisions: It had never done so; it had never needed to.[39]

Despite these uncertainties, the activation of Article Five was an historic moment, one that was sadly underappreciated by the Bush administration and particularly by the U.S. military, which viewed possible joint military action with Europeans in Afghanistan as more a potential "nuisance" than anything else.[40] Nonetheless, NATO's vote showed a new awareness of the meaning of terrorism: Article Five was originally intended to draw all of Western Europe and North America to the common defense in the event of a Soviet attack, and had never been used in the Alliance's 52 year history until that moment.

Invoking Article Five did not automatically guarantee the use of force, and French and German leaders in particular showed a certain amount of reticence about the possibility of military action. (French president Jacques Chirac was reluctant even to use the word "war.")[41] By contrast, British Prime Minister Tony Blair, who would become Bush's closest ally both in retaliating against Afghanistan and preventively attacking Iraq, recalled 9/11 as "a revelation":

What had seemed inchoate came together. The point about September 11th was not its detailed planning; not its devilish execution; not even, simply, that it happened in America, on the streets of New York. All of this made it an astonishing, terrible and wicked tragedy, a barbaric murder of innocent people. But what galvanized me was that *it was a declaration of war* by religious fanatics who were prepared to wage that war without limit. They killed 3000. But if they could have killed 30,000 or 300,000 they would have rejoiced in it. The purpose was to cause such hatred between Moslems and the West that a religious jihad became reality; and the world engulfed by it. (emphasis added)

"From September 11th on," Blair continued, "I could see the threat plainly. Here were terrorists prepared to bring about Armageddon." He also shared Aznar's lack of confidence in notions like containment. "Containment will not work in the face of the global threat that confronts us. The terrorists have no intention of being contained."[42]

Even if other European leaders were not willing to talk about war as bluntly as Bush or Blair, the United States and Europe still shared a new sense of danger. As one European security analyst later noted, 9/11 created a consensus in NATO about the threat, if not the solution:

The urgency of the threat was clear, as was, for the most part, its definition. [NATO] agreed that terrorism was not a conventional threat; that it was more often than not driven by groups and individuals, not governments; and that it may not be defeated by traditional means such as deterrence. . . . But the post-9/11 consensus within NATO had its limits. It covered the diagnosis but not the cure.[43]

The traumatic recognition that deterrence might no longer protect the West from attack would eventually lead NATO, in the words of American analysts Ivo Daalder and James Goldgeier, to "go global," expanding its military reach and perhaps at some point considering the addition of new members outside Europe. This reflected a recognition that terrorism is not a specifically a transatlantic phenomenon; as Daalder and Goldgeier put it, terrorists "born in Riyadh and trained in Kandahar hatch deadly plots in Hamburg to fly airplanes into buildings in New York."[44] This sense has not yet resulted in an explicit NATO doctrine of prevention, but there has been clear evolution in Atlantic thinking away from deterrence and toward more active measures since 9/11.

In retrospect, it should not be surprising that terrorism made so rapid a transition in so many people's minds from a police problem to a military conflict. Although 9/11 was a terrible shock to the international community, it was really only the most grandiose of a series of increasingly aggressive and spectacular plots by terrorists of various political stripes around the world, some of which came to pass, others which were thwarted. These included the first World Trade Center bombing in 1993, a plot to crash airliners into the Eiffel Tower in 1994, the poison gas attack against the Japanese subway system in 1995, attempted bombings of Jewish neighborhoods in Canada in the late 1990s, and many others. With 9/11, terrorism finally came to be seen not as a disorganized series of horrible incidents, but a means of warfare being used by an actual movement, "the method of choice," as George Shultz put it, "of an extensive, internationally connected ideological movement dedicated to the destruction of our international system of cooperation and progress."[45]

Treating terrorism as a protracted war rather than as an international criminal problem has deep ramifications. At the least, it means rejecting the traditional mechanisms of law enforcement, with their long delays and risks that the offender might go free, as unacceptable given the new stakes and risks. Where deterrence is concerned, it means that any hope the enemy could be prevented from going to war has been overtaken by the assumption that the enemy has *already* gone to war and that deterrence, insofar as it mattered at all, has already failed.

In turn, confidence in the ability to induce restraint in potential foes gives way to risk-minimizing assumptions that rogues and terrorists relentlessly intend to do harm and will do so unless physically stopped. Tony Blair made such a claim directly a year after the Iraq war, when he defended U.S. and British preventive military action against Saddam and chided those who had argued for more time for other measures:

And my judgment then and now is that the risk of this new global terrorism and its interaction with states or organizations or individuals proliferating WMD, is one I simply am not prepared to run. This is not a time to err on the side of caution; not a time to weigh the risks to an infinite balance; not a time for the cynicism of the worldly wise who favor playing it long. Their worldly wise cynicism is actually at best naiveté and at worst dereliction.[46]

Statements like these are a response to increased risk and uncertainty in international life. "We live in a world of old rules and new threats," wrote former Clinton administration official Lee Feinstein and Princeton professor Anne-Marie Slaughter in late 2003. "This period did not begin on September 11, 2001."[47] But the solution to these threats is less clear, and how to deal with them has become the center of international debate, with traditional strategies of deterrence now pitted against calls for a more active defense.

Deterrence Versus Prevention

In recent years, and especially since 9/11, the perception of terrorism as a challenge to the international status quo rather than as a criminal nuisance has grown in tandem with increasing fears about the role of rogue states—who, like terrorists, are by their nature challengers to the status quo—in nuclear and other weapons proliferation. Thus the debate over whether to strike terrorists preventively has become increasingly intertwined with a similar debate about whether it might be acceptable to engage in preventive attacks on rogue nuclear forces—or, in a combined threat, in preventive war against regimes that may serve as the nexus between terrorist organizations and the sources of weapons of mass destruction. This, of course, was the initial American rationale for the 2003 Gulf War.

Less than a year after 9/11, Yale law professor Ruth Wedgwood would allude to just how much international norms, including the aversion to relying on deterrence, had changed. "If [the] question is, is it legal to use force to prevent a country from acquiring a weapon of mass destruction, in the old days people would have said no," Wedgwood said in early 2002. But she pointed out that there was now a "different sensibility" afoot, especially in light of Saddam Hussein's behavior at the time.[48] Whether reasonable or not, what were once separate anxieties about terrorism, rogue states, and proliferation have now become woven in the minds of many people into a single tapestry representing a nearly existential level of danger.

Foreign policy scholar Robert Lieber, for example, explicitly linked these two debates in late 2006: "The phenomenon of radical Islamism, coupled with terrorism and the specter of weapons of mass destruction, poses a long-term danger to all Western societies, and there is no separate peace to be had."[49] Jurist Richard Posner likewise drew a similar link in arguing that the American legal system must adapt to a new security environment:

in the early days of the twenty-first century, the nation faces the intertwined menaces of global terrorism and proliferation of weapons of mass destruction. A city can be destroyed by an atomic bomb the size of a melon, which if coated in lead would be undetectable. Large stretches of a city can be rendered uninhabitable, perhaps for decades, merely by the explosion of a conventional bomb that has been coated with radioactive material. . . . Our terrorist enemies have the will to do such things and abundant opportunities. . . . The problem of proliferation is more serious today than it was in what now seem the almost halcyon days of the Cold War; it will be even more serious tomorrow.[50]

These kinds of beliefs, as will be seen in the following chapter, are not limited to Americans. The combined pressures of proliferation and the emergence of large-scale suicide terrorism have, in many quarters, clearly shaken entrenched beliefs about deterrence and rationality in international affairs.

But why should this be so? Are the new threats so "new" that they demand radically different policies? After all, more than three decades ago, Israeli scholar Yehezkel Dror had already posited the problem of "crazy states," deeply aggressive nations, perhaps led by fanatics or dictators (or both) who are ideologically driven and prone to almost insanely risky gambles.[51] Nor are fears of proliferation all that new: as Betts pointed out just before the 2003 Gulf War, the U.S. did not attack China as it crossed the nuclear threshold, even though Mao Zedong was once thought to be "as fanatically aggressive and crazy as Saddam."[52] Likewise, Stanley Hoffmann criticized the Bush administration's fears that WMD in the hands of rogue states might serve to "deter the U.S. and [in turn] make American deterrence impossible," arguing that these are fears "that nothing in our past experience with the USSR and China justifies."[53]

What makes the world so much more frightening today than when it was menaced by the supposedly undeterrable old men of the former Soviet Kremlin or the Chinese communist fanatics of the early Cold War?

One obvious answer is the emergence of non-state organizations willing to engage in mass suicide terrorism, such as al-Qaeda. Suicide terrorism, by its very nature, defeats the logic of deterrence itself, since the enemy wants no concession or solution, and will not act to save his own life or even to ensure the survival of his nation.[54] Nor is negotiation possible; if scholar Daniel Byman is correct that "al-Qaeda seeks America's unconditional surrender," there is little that can be offered short of lay-ing down arms and accepting the enemy's terms.[55] Former NATO Secretary General Lord George Robertson has referred to this kind of threat as a "special breed of terrorism," which is "driven not by achievable political aims, but by fanatical extremism and the urge to kill."[56] This would be less of a worry if it were not for the technological advancements that can now allow terrorists to inflict damage far out of proportion to their actual size. Relying on deterrence in such an environment is especially dangerous; as John Gaddis has emphasized, "deterrence against states affords insufficient protection from attacks by gangs, which can now inflict the kind of damage only states fighting wars used to be able to achieve."[57]

Another change is that closed, paranoid states like totalitarian North Korea, theocratic Iran, and now-vanquished Baathist Iraq are no longer being held in check by the constraints of the Cold War and the close supervision of former patrons like the United States, China, and the Soviet Union. (Whatever their other sins, the Soviets were actually fairly consistent in their determination to prevent the spread of nuclear technology.) Moreover, with the collapse of the Soviet bloc, terrorist groups that once found shelter in Eastern Europe have scattered and been left to their own irresponsible devices—a paradoxical benefit of the Cold War's end that deprived terrorists of training and financing but also made them more difficult to track and restrain. All these actors, state and non-state, have sought weapons of mass destruction, including nuclear arms and, in the case of North Korea and Iran, the means to deliver them directly to American or allied territory by long-range missiles.

But one of the most powerful factors in helping to erode the credibility of deterrence has been the behavior of rogues and terrorists themselves. Because terrorists and rogues are fundamentally opponents of the international status quo, they do not have a vested interest in its stability. Indeed, they may actually seek to *create* crises rather than to resolve them, springing surprises and making daring moves in an effort to alter or transform the system, as North Korea did with its sudden and risky 2006 nuclear test and its provocative series of missile launches earlier the same year, or as al-Qaeda did in its surprise attack on 9/11. This unreliability and unpredictability provides a strong incentive to strike preventively, rather than to trust in deterrence, since trusting in deterrence might mean having to trust in unverifiable agreements, in the rationality and stability of aggressive and perhaps even unhinged dictators, and in negotiation and diplomacy—a path increasingly discredited by long years of duplicitous and cynical Iraqi, Iranian, and North Korean behavior. Especially worrisome is that it could mean having to trust in the unproven deterrability of terrorists who believe that engaging in mass murder and instigating a global religious war will secure them an eternity cavorting with virgins in Paradise and who therefore not only seek no compromise or resolution, but welcome conflict and chaos.

This is the very crux of the deterrence dilemma: if the enemy seeks nothing, or at least nothing that the target can give, has nothing to protect or save, and intends only to inflict death at any cost, then relying on deterrence means little more than ceding the initiative to the enemy and suffering the inevitable attack at some point. Deterrence by its nature is reactive: as strategist Colin Gray points out, a "policy that seeks security through deterrence knowingly concedes the vital power of decision to the foe."

Only the putative enemy can decide whether or not he is deterred. No matter how fearsome our military might, or how awesome our reputation for carrying through on our contingent military threats, the success or otherwise of our policy of deterrence is decided only by the other side. There is nothing, repeat nothing, we can do to assure deterrence.[58]

This kind of reliance on the enemy was nerve-wracking enough during the Cold War, but it was at least reasonable to presume that the Soviet leadership did not want to incinerate themselves along with most of the rest of civilization. But there is no way around the central point, which is that deterrence shifts the initiative, the very decision to go to war itself, into the hands of the enemy. In the worst case, relying on the comforting thought that deterrence is working may in reality only provide more time to an enemy plotting his next move. If the opponent is actually seeking conflict, then adopting a deterrent strategy may not only fail to keep the peace, it might actually hasten its end. *New York Times* editor Bill Keller has summed up this paradox succinctly: "In the short run, war is perilous. But in the long run peace can be a killer, too."[59]

Deterrence is an especially difficult calculation when faced with a leader or regime who values something more than life, or even national survival. A 2006 RAND study suggested that the existence of such actors is the central cause of skepticism, at least in the United States, about deterrence:

[D]eterrence and defense (using both military and nonmilitary means) appear to offer less adequate protection against some types of security threats than they once did—or, more accurately, the sorts of threats against which they provide the least reliable protection now loom larger than they did in past decades. The perceived inadequacy of deterrence relates primarily to facing adversaries whose actions are not amenable to deterrence because they value nothing more than attacking the United States, or because the United States simply has little or no ability to influence their behavior.

While the RAND authors acknowledge that this kind of reasoning "might change under a subsequent [U.S.] presidential administration," other factors tempting decision makers to preventive solutions "are likely to persist as long as the current security environment obtains."[60] Such actors could see large-scale destruction as virtuous, even at the cost of a nation. This would be particularly worrisome if "the adversary was seen not as a secular opponent, but as a transcendental evil or pagan force whose eradication was considered theologically permissible and morally correct."[61] When faced with enemies schooled in a culture of martyrdom, or regimes led by paranoid or even delusional leaders, it is not difficult to see why the reliance on deterrence is increasingly coming into question in the developed world.

Another problem unique to the twenty-first century is that trusting deterrence may come down to trusting in the sanity and reasonableness of a single person. While the president of the United States and the chairman of the Soviet Communist Party both held the codes to launch nuclear weapons, each side had bureaucratic and military checks in place to ensure that a single madman could not initiate Armageddon. Even Stalin had advisors and generals to whom he turned in wartime, and an argument could be made that restrictions on the ability of later Soviet leaders to launch nuclear war were even better than those on their U.S. counterparts. Do such checks exist, say, in North Korea, to restrain a leader whose composite description by some who have met him is a "vain, paranoid, cognac-guzzling hypochondriac"?[62] Osama bin Laden did not hesitate to orchestrate the murder of nearly three thousand people in a day. Would he be more reticent to kill three million? No one knows, and this uncertainty helps to make preventive action, with all its attendant risks, seem more attractive than trusting in the reason, sanity, or values of any one particular leader.

And so the nature of the enemy in the twenty-first century is itself another factor draining faith in deterrence as a workable defense. During the Cold War, the consequences of a failure of deterrence would have been horrible beyond all human comprehension. Although the superpowers held each other's nations hostage, they generally did their best to avoid any crisis that could touch off war; even when they were willing to use force, they went to great lengths to avoid a nuclear showdown, and "crisis management" became one of the standard phrases of the Cold War. Terrorists and rogues, however, may actually seek to create crises and to launch their own "bolts from the blue" as they did on 9/11. This unreliability and unpredictability is cited by proponents of preventive attack as justification for striking far in advance of any obvious threat, not least because such advocates argue that waiting until an actual, visible threat has materialized will only mean it is too late to stop it.

A Note on "Imminence"

The question of how firmly a threat has to coalesce before action can be taken against it raises one very important part of the deterrence equation that has come into question in the post-Cold War era, and has never been all that clearly defined in any case. This is the concept of *imminence.*

If preemption is interpreted as a kind of spoiling attack against an enemy who is about to strike first, it is permissible only because such an attack is "imminent"; that is, there is no realistic alternative but to strike or be struck. (This is derived from the so-called "*Caroline* test" noted in Chapter 1.)[63] Of course this is a rubbery term that could mean, as one legal scholar has wryly noted, "any one of several things—an hour, day, week, year, or decade."[64] But the basic concept is simple enough: by international law and custom, violence is only permissible after deterrence has failed, or perhaps more precisely, is in the process of failing, and national leaders have a reasonable expectation that aggression against their interests is unavoidable. This normally means tangible evidence, and not just empty threats, of impending military action, perhaps even only within days or weeks.

Given the potential destructiveness of a terrorist or rogue attack, however, and the stealth by which it might be delivered, this traditional understanding of imminence has been revisited in the debate regarding deterrence and preemption. Some legal scholars, for example, have argued that "imminence" must be detached from a strictly temporal meaning. John Yoo, a Berkeley law professor who served in the G. W.

Bush Justice Department, has argued that imminence must be redefined as a kind of matrix of threats, including

> an analysis that goes beyond the temporal proximity of a threat to include the probability that the threat will occur. In addition to the probability of the threat, the threatened magnitude of harm must be relevant. The advent of nuclear and other sophisticated weapons has dramatically increased the degree of potential harm, and the importance of the temporal factor has diminished.[65]

In other words, the key consideration is whether waiting until a threat is "imminent" as traditionally understood means that any possible action to oppose it is unlikely to succeed.[66] Although Yoo's analysis is clearly an attempt to place the Bush administration's invasion of Iraq in a more solid legal framework, his call for a revision in legal norms has been echoed by other legal scholars as well. Anthony Arend, for one, worries that "with nuclear weapons or other weapons of mass destruction, by the time the [*Caroline*] test is met, it is probably too late."[67]

As with other aspects of the prevention debate, the problem of imminence is not as novel as it may seem. As early as 1977, ethicist Michael Walzer argued that the concept of imminence, at least as embodied in the *Caroline* test, was pointlessly restrictive, and if strictly observed would "permit us only to do little more than respond to an attack *once we had seen it coming* but before we had felt its impact" (emphasis original).[68] Walzer offers a more permissive interpretation:

> The line between legitimate and illegitimate first strikes is not going to be drawn at the point of *imminent attack* but at the point of *sufficient threat*. That phrase is necessarily vague. I mean it to cover three things: a manifest intent to injure, a degree of active preparation that makes that intent a positive danger, and a general situation in which waiting, or doing anything other than fighting, greatly magnifies the risk. (emphasis added)[69]

Walzer's proposal unavoidably (and intentionally) blurs the traditional distinction between prevention and preemption. But this is no academic exercise: if the international community today were to adopt Walzer's 1977 criteria, a host of actions that were previously of questionable legitimacy would become positively acceptable. An Israeli strike against Iran's nuclear program, for example, could conceivably meet all three of Walzer's tests, although interestingly, the U.S. invasion of Iraq would fail all of them except perhaps an "intent to injure."

Critics, of course, find this position dubious at best, and at worst a rationalization for the exercise of violence at will. They would argue that, at the very least, action taken without clear signs of impending aggression, if not the danger of "imminent" hostilities, is illegal under current international law.[70] Others fear that acting based only on suspicions—particularly based on partial or ambiguous evidence—will encourage others to do the same and create a kind of international free-for-all. States, in this scenario, both abandon the concept of imminence and forgo the reassurances of deterrence, and instead choose actions that in the short term might seem decisive and final, but in the long term prove to be destabilizing and even more dangerous in some ways than the threat against which they were originally aimed.

These unresolved legal and precedential issues will occupy international lawyers for some time to come. But it is likely that these legal questions will in any case soon be overtaken by state practice, as international law so often is.

However, before leaving the issue of imminence specifically and deterrence generally, there are historical precedents worth considering for a moment that bear upon both concepts. While it is true that preventive war is still technically illegal, states can in fact legitimately practice "anticipatory self-defense." This has already been discussed as "preemption," the attack against an aggressor who is about to strike. In contrast to preventive war, "anticipatory self-defense" is a "narrower doctrine that would authorize armed responses to attacks that are on the brink of launch, or where an enemy attack has already occurred and the victim learns more attacks are planned."[71] But the actual practice of "anticipatory self-defense" is a bit more complicated, and reveals that the border between preemption and prevention is less a bright and clear line than legal scholars might like. It also suggests that reliance on deterrence, at least where certain kinds of regimes are concerned, was weakening long before 9/11.

In 1986, for example, in the wake of a Libyan bomb plot in Germany that killed two American servicemen, the United States invoked anticipatory self-defense when it conducted air strikes against Libya to forestall future terrorist attacks. Although several countries sponsored a UN resolution condemning the U.S. attack, Australia, the UK, Denmark, and even France—which actually opposed the Libyan raid and refused to cooperate with the Americans in executing it—opposed the resolution.[72] In 1993, the Clinton administration bombed targets in Iraq in response to evidence that Saddam Hussein had attempted to kill former president

George H. W. Bush. The American rationale was to influence the Iraqi regime "to cease planning future attacks against the United States," although no evidence was presented of such impending attacks. The Security Council declined the demands of the Iraqis to condemn the U.S. action.[73] In 1998, the Security Council took no action on the Clinton administration's attack on a Sudanese factory which the Americans claimed was making components for nerve gas, nor did it censure U.S. strikes on suspected terrorist training sites in Afghanistan.

The point here is not that whether these were wise or prudent actions, or even whether they were grounded in any kind of real threat. (Reagan's Libyan bombing and Clinton's attack in response to the plot against the elder Bush, for example, could easily be interpreted as acts of revenge rather than self-defense, whatever their actual motivation.) More important is that they show that the international community, by the 1980s, had already moved toward more acceptance of actions meant to sidestep the uncertainties of deterrence where rogues and terrorists were concerned. Secretary of State George Shultz defended American actions in 1986 by claiming that it was "absurd to argue that international law prohibits us from capturing terrorists in international waters or airspace; from attacking them on the soil of other nations, even for the purpose of rescuing hostages; or from using force against states that support, train, and harbor terrorists or guerrillas."[74] As Canadian legal scholar Michael Byers has noted, at the time Shultz's claim was "widely rejected by other states," but within fifteen years the secretary's formulation became customary international law.[75] Likewise, the international system seems to be in a similar period of change, as the doubts about deterrence that surfaced during the establishment of the so-called Shultz Doctrine have significantly deepened in the wake of the Cold War's end and the ensuing terrorist mayhem wreaked on New York, Washington, Moscow, London, Madrid, and other places.

After 9/11, the concept of "anticipatory self-defense" took on a greater salience in international life. The nature and destructiveness of the terrorist attacks of 2001 and after raised the question of just how long a state would have to wait, how much information its intelligence services needed to have, or how much warning could be discerned, before it would be permissible to disrupt the enemy's preparations. This uncertainty was compounded by the unsettling realization that future enemies may not signal their intent to strike in ways that could be understood, even if they cared to send such a message in the first place. The cultural and ideological, and even geographical, disconnect between the West and its enemies has never been greater, and this too raises fears that the old rules of international conflict are no longer useful or relevant. "My God, it emerged from Afghanistan," former U.S. national security advisor Brent Scowcroft said of 9/11 shortly after the attacks, "just about the most backward forgotten country on the planet. It shows how little we know about where the threats are coming from."[76] He might have added that it also shows how little we know about how to deter them.

Although it seems in retrospect that the Americans and several other UN members have for some time now shown a readiness to permit preventive (or at the least, highly "anticipatory") actions against particular actors or targets, if only on an ad hoc basis, this was never translated explicitly into national policy in the United States or anywhere else until the twenty-first century. The exceptions, in a sense, honored the rule, and while the great powers reserved the right to act against international law and traditional norms in their own interests, they did so in what Gilles Andréani has called a kind of "Catholic" manner: they accepted that they were sinning, and might sin again, but accepted their actions as sins nevertheless. Andréani believes this approach has served the international community reasonably well, by preserving norms against the discretionary use of force while still leaving room for nations to act in their own defense.[77]

But like many sins before it, Catholic or otherwise, the sin of prevention is rapidly losing its status as a mortal vice. And while it might never be proclaimed as good or desirable, many nations no longer seem willing to repent of it, and some, as will be seen in the next chapter, are choosing to embrace it as necessary, if not exactly virtuous.

Chapter 4
International Perspectives on Preemption and Prevention

As for carrying out preventive strikes against terrorist bases . . . we will take all measures to liquidate terrorist bases in any region of the world

—General Yurii Baluyevski, Russian General Staff, 2004

The vast majority of Japanese agree that we need to be able to carry out first strikes.

—Japanese professor Yoichi Shimada, 2006

NATO has now recognized that the best (and at times the only) defense against . . . remote dangers is to tackle them at their source.

—Ivo Daalder and James Goldgeier, 2006

There is more going on here than the United States going its own way through the aspirations of one particular administration. For a variety of reasons, many states in diverse parts of the world support a more liberal use of violence to curb terrorists and mitigate the risk that rogue states may assist them.

—Canadian legal scholar Mark Drumbl, 2003

Ethiopia's Christmas War

On Christmas Eve 2006, Ethiopia launched a series of strikes against neighboring Somalia, with whom it had fought at least two wars over the past years, primarily over territory. This time, however, borders were not the issue. The capital, Mogadishu, and much of Somalia had fallen under the control of the Union of Islamic Courts, a paramilitary organization which claimed to want to bring Islamic law to the disorder in the country, but which its opponents, including the United States, believed had larger goals beyond the immediate chaos in Somalia, including possible links to al-Qaeda. Both Ethiopia and the official Somali govern-ment—which was recognized by the United Nations but was unable on its own to control any significant territory—charged that the Courts were bringing foreign fighters into the Horn of Africa in the service of broader revolutionary plans in the region.

The Ethiopians decided to take no chances, and chose to head off the creation of a fundamentalist Islamic regime on their border. "The Ethiopian government is bombing non-civilian targets in Somalia in order to disable and prevent the delivery of arms and supplies to the Islamic courts," an advisor to the Ethiopian prime minister announced. The prime minister himself later declared: "Our defense force has been forced to enter a war to defend against the attacks from extremists and anti-Ethiopian forces and to protect the sovereignty of the land. Our intention is to win this war as soon as possible."[1] And win they did: the official Somali government, backed by Ethiopian jets, tanks, and infan-try, marched into Mogadishu within a few days. Islamic fighters fled the area, discarding their skullcaps and shaving their beards in attempts to blend into the population.[2] Al-Qaeda leaders, showing their usual tone-deafness to international politics, promptly issued a call for the defeated Islamic fighters to engage in terror tactics, which many Somali Islamists in turn promptly vowed to heed, thus inadvertently vindicating the origi-nal charge that the Islamic Courts had at least terrorist sympathies, if not formal connections.[3]

Whether this Ethiopian intervention will finally bring order to Soma-lia is doubtful, as thousands of Islamic fighters remain active in the region as of this writing. But more striking than the intervention itself is that it took place not with the official approval of any regional organiza-tion, and certainly not with the sanction of the United Nations Security Council—which, as usual, could not reach a consensus on the issue even as Ethiopian forces pressed toward Mogadishu—but instead with the tacit approval of many African and Western countries, the United States foremost among them.[4] Rather than tolerate a gathering threat, the Ethiopians unilaterally took matters into their own hands and dispersed a would-be regime in a neighboring country in the name of their own national security, with the approval of many important members of the international community.

The Ethiopian strike against the Islamic Courts in 2006 was just one example of the growing and increasingly global rise of preventive think-ing. Many nations are openly contemplating and debating policies aimed at neutralizing, rather than deterring, their enemies, and preventing potential threats from coalescing into actual dangers. The Americans were naturally among the most prominent supporters of the Ethiopian attack on the Islamic Courts, since the Americans were among the first to proclaim an explicit right to engage in preventive violence.[5] But the United States has not been the last nor, as it turns out, even the most vehement, advocate of prevention.

The question of international attitudes on the issue of prevention is a crucial one. If other nations are decisively rejecting notions of prevention and defending traditional norms regarding the use of force, then U.S. policy in the early twenty-first century might well come to be seen in the near future—perhaps as early, say, as January 2009, when George Bush leaves office—as an anomaly. But if other nations are expressing the kinds of anxieties voiced by the Americans, then something larger is afoot. When even the Vatican starts talking about "the need for prompt intervention, indeed prevention of acts of terrorism," as Pope John Paul II's foreign secretary did in 2004, it should be clear that something important is changing in the international community.[6]

Still, when Washington speaks, its voice can be one of the loudest indeed in the international community, and in 2002 it issued a blunt and vocal rejection of previous international norms.

The U.S. National Security Strategy and Its Critics

In late 2002, the administration of President George W. Bush released its edition of the National Security Strategy of the United States of America (NSS), a series of documents required by American law and produced (albeit irregularly) in every presidential administration since 1986. The NSS is supposed to be a report to Congress on the state of America's national security, but in reality previous iterations have tended to be restatements of a president's goals, achievements, and general policies. They are, in the main, unremarkable, and usually were issued without significant public notice or reaction.

But one year after 9/11, the White House issued a revised NSS that represented a significant departure from previous reports in both tone and substance. Gone were boilerplate restatements of administration policy, replaced instead by steely warnings that the United States would no longer tolerate the chaos and consequent dangers of the new century.

The sections that gained the most attention and the most intense criticism were those that stated that the U.S. will no longer wait to be struck first, but will actively seek to attack enemies before they can become a threat:

While the United States will constantly strive to enlist the support of the international community, we will not hesitate to act alone, if necessary, to exercise our right of self defense by acting preemptively against such terrorists, to prevent them from doing harm against our people and our country. . . .

We must be prepared to stop rogue states and their terrorist clients before they are able to threaten or use weapons of mass destruction against the United States and our allies and friends . . . .To forestall or prevent such hostile acts by our adversaries, the United States will, if necessary, act preemptively.[7]

In a matter of a few pages, U.S. policy officially shifted from reliance on traditional notions of deterrence toward a theory of prevention, regardless of the garbled attempt to camouflage it under more acceptable language about preemption. Although it is arguable to what extent prevention could be called a "new" strategy, its elevation from a desperate act of last resort to just another military option—and perhaps even a first resort—represented a major shift in emphasis. In any case, even if preventive concepts were not new, such frank statements about them from a U.S. administration were. One American defense analyst later wrote, "what is new is [the] open discussion" about prevention, if not the actual options themselves.[8]

Both at home and abroad, the reaction to the assertion of prevention as a right of self-defense was predictably negative—not least because it was coming from the most powerful country in the world, whose might and resources could plausibly transform such an assertion into an actual strategy. Critics expressed concerns that the new American stance was in fact an aggressive repudiation of previous notions of self-defense, and that its impact on the international community would be strong enough to alter traditional presumptions against the resort to violence.[9] American scholar G. John Ikenberry even argued that the Bush administration had adopted a "neoimperial grand strategy" that not only undermined American security but threatened "to rend the fabric of the international community."[10]

Others were less alarmed, but still critical. One 2003 analysis suggested that the international objections to the so-called "Bush Doctrine" showed that the whole business had backfired and that protests against the Bush administration's move toward prevention served to illustrate the limits, rather than the reach, of American influence. The authors contended that The United States "has been served notice that its tremendous material power is insufficient to alter global political understandings."[11] But this did not quell concerns like those of historian Paul Schroeder, who wrote that a "more dangerous, illegitimate norm and example can hardly be imagined . . . .This is not a theoretical or academic point."[12]

This anxiety about emulation was widespread. Just before the invasion of Iraq, a Chinese scholar wrote:

Adopting a preemptive strategy sets a bad example for other governments and could have a seriously negative global impact. If the U.S. example were to be followed, Israel could launch preemptive attacks against Palestine or other Arab countries, and India and Pakistan could launch preemptive strikes against each other. By acting on its goal of eliminating the supposed threat of Iraqi WMD, therefore, the United States would increase the potential for more military conflicts, making the world even more insecure and unstable.[13]

Even those who admired some aspects of the NSS, as a team of Brookings Institution scholars did in 2002, expressed fears that other nations might "embrace the preemption argument as a cover for settling their own national security scores."[14] Henry Kissinger likewise warned in 2002 that it "cannot be in either the American national interest or the world's interest to develop principles that grant every nation an unfettered right of preemption against its own definition of threats to its security."[15]

More practical objections centered less on whether the Bush Doctrine was legitimate or whether it would be emulated, but rather that it was something of a pipe dream. Critics like strategist Andrew Bacevich argued that the sweeping breadth of the NSS is predicated on a belief that American resources are unlimited, and that such a doctrine would therefore be almost impossible to execute—a criticism that seems rather more salient as the United States heads toward a decade of involvement in Iraq.[16] But these operational issues were of less concern to those who feared that the Americans were single-handedly tearing apart the existing international order. Stanley Hoffmann spoke for many such critics in June 2003 when he bluntly charged that a strategy of prevention is "a recipe for turning the world into a jungle."[17]

Where the issue of changing international norms is concerned, there are two general assumptions underlying most criticisms of the 2002

National Security Strategy (which was reissued with essentially the same language in 2006). One is the idea that the preventive emphasis in the National Security Strategy was radically new, perhaps reflecting an American overreaction to 9/11. The other is that the explicit embrace of preventive solutions was somehow peculiar to the United States, and that such solutions are fundamentally rejected by the other major actors in the international community. The Bush administration's doctrine of "preventive" self-defense, American legal scholar Hurst Hannum charged in 2003, "is rejected by everyone but State Department lawyers whose job it is to defend the positions of their client."[18]

But neither assumption is accurate. As discussed previously, consideration of preventive options in the United States began in earnest in the early 1990s, spurred initially not by terrorist attacks but by the larger problem of instability left in the wake of the Cold War. As the Brookings group noted in discussing the 2002 NSS, there was a certain amount of amnesia among those who worried that the Bush Doctrine represented some sort of dramatic change, especially given that only four years earlier the Clinton administration had attacked targets in Sudan and Afghanistan on explicitly preventive grounds.[19] Historian Melvyn Leffler calls it "lovely nostalgia" to think that Clinton's policies were much different from Bush's, although he echoes European critics that Bush's mistake was to "translate an option into a national doctrine."[20] Moreover, such discussions were never limited to U.S. policy circles. Other nations were, and are, no less interested than the United States in seeking new options to counter new threats, including the use of preventive violence.

The International Rise of Prevention: "The French Are Not from Venus"

None of this is to say that other nations necessarily admire American theories of preventive war, especially in the wake of the array of unconscionable blunders made before and after the invasion of Iraq. But there have always been more problems in the world than Iraq, many of which are seen in foreign capitals as more threatening than anything Saddam Hussein might have been cooking up in the shadows of his palaces. American researchers Peter Dombrowski and Rodger Payne, both of whom have been firm critics of the Bush Doctrine, have pointed out:

In the wake of the horrible 9/11, Madrid, and Beslan [Russia] terrorist attacks, [foreign] national leaders are more and more declaring their disinterest in absorbing such strikes and then finding and prosecuting the perpetrators after the fact. Like the Bush administration, many national leaders call for new approaches to meet the new threat. Cold war era retaliatory policies, which embraced the logic of deterrence, are increasingly disparaged and renounced.[21]

Foreign observers agree, particularly in Europe. Brussels-based analyst Tomas Valasek wrote in 2003 that "many European countries have gone through a thought process very similar to Washington's. The belief that pre-9/11 defense strategies do not correspond to new security threats— threats not only to the United States but also to Europe—is reflected in the national security documents of the key European states."[22] French strategist François Heisbourg agrees, noting that France and other European nations may be less likely to shrink from military options in highly threatening situations than their rhetoric might suggest, even if their threshold for action could well be higher than Washington's. While the current perception abroad might be that the Americans, so to speak, are from Mars, Heisbourg warns that "the French are not from Venus," a comment that could apply to other major powers as well.[23]

To some extent, this shift toward prevention is due to the unpredictable nature of threats from groups like al-Qaeda. Rather than draw distinctions among Western targets, al-Qaeda and associated Islamist groups have made a series of indiscriminate threats against a variety of countries regardless of their regimes or foreign policies. From a strategic point of view, these threats are often incomprehensible and even foolish; they seem to reflect a diffuse, overarching fury against the entire West that only reinforces beliefs about the relentlessness of the enemy and the inevitability of attack, and this in turn has led to an increasing sense of anxiety and insecurity, particularly in Europe.

Despite French and German opposition to the U.S.-led war in Iraq, for example, Islamists have nonetheless targeted both nations for attack. A 2006 al-Qaeda call for violence against France led the chief of French domestic security to note that the threat of terror was "very high and very international," and that as far as France's "Islamist adversaries" were concerned, the Republic was "in the Western camp . . . and we will be spared nothing."[24] The discovery of a bomb plot against the German train system likewise led to a sharp increase in the number of Germans who felt themselves under threat, and prompted one German politician to echo a line more often heard from more hawkish Americans: "It's not what we do, it's who we are that makes us a target."[25]

This sense of threat is not limited to the United States and Western Europe. Canada—again, despite its opposition to the invasion of Iraq and the serious breach in U.S.-Canadian relations it caused—learned that it, too, was not to be spared from mass terror. In 2006 Canadian security forces broke up a plot among a group of Canadian Muslims to blow up Parliament and behead the prime minister, thus "shattering," the *Economist* noted, "an article of faith among Canadians . . . that their commitment to an easygoing multicultural society protects them from home-grown Islamist terrorism."[26] The father of one of the men accused in the plot later complained that Canada "is supposed to be a free and democratic society. You are supposed to be innocent until proven guilty." But Canada, the *Economist* writers dryly noted, "was also supposed to be a country where the prime minister ran no risk of losing his head."

At times, the hatred of organizations like al-Qaeda can seem almost inexplicably random, and therefore even more broadly threatening. In 2003, for example, an al-Qaeda communiqué threatened action, for some unknown reason, against Norway. Norwegian officials were completely baffled; Oslo is not only considered something of an honest broker in the Middle East, but with the exception of its membership in NATO and a very small contingent of special forces troops at the time in Afghanistan, Norway would not normally have been considered a target for Islamist violence. The threat was in fact so weird that the Norwegians wondered if the al-Qaeda planners simply couldn't read a map properly. An unnamed Norwegian diplomat told the BBC that it was the hope of the Norwegian authorities "that al-Qaeda simply got their geography wrong and did not mean to threaten Norway at all."[27]

But while these kinds of threats have played a role in forcing many nations to reconsider traditional notions of deterrence and security since 2001, and especially after the launching of the Iraq war in 2003, the changes in Western defense policies may not be as novel as they seem. Dana Allin of the International Institute of Strategic Studies in London has suggested that attitudes, at least in the major European states and America, were more or less "converging" on issues of prevention even before 9/11. Kosovo, Allin points out, was in essence a preventive war, and NATO operations against the Taliban in Afghanistan after 9/11 had a strong preventive component to them as well.[28] Heisbourg also notes an international evolution in the late 1990s from strategies of "soft" prevention, which rely on diplomatic and other nonviolent instruments, such as sanctions, toward more interest in "hard" prevention, although not necessarily of the unilateral variety favored by the Americans.[29] "There are signs," he wrote in 2003, "that preemption can and has already begun to be incorporated into other countries' national defense strategies;" in 2006 he acknowledged that "preemption" in these strategies is increasingly coming closer to what would normally be understood as prevention.[30]

The Israeli Exception

Israel is the most obvious example of a country that openly embraces prevention. The Jewish state has long practiced both preemption and prevention against various threats, both real and potential, to its security, in operations ranging from outright acts of war, such as invading Lebanon or launching an air raid against an Iraqi nuclear facility, to smaller scale operations such as "targeted killings" of terrorists in various locations.[31] Israel over the years has remained an unapologetic advocate of prevention, most recently where Iran's seemingly unstoppable nuclear program is concerned. But even these warnings about the Iranians are actually only the continuation of a longstanding preventive policy, publicly declared in 1981 by prime minister Menachem Begin, that "nuclear weapons must not be in the possession of Arabs" or other states hostile to Israel, including Iran.[32] In 2003 Israel's defense minister warned that "under no circumstances would Israel be able to tolerate nuclear weapons in Iranian possession," and in 2006 the prime minister again declared that Israel refused to rule out military action if the Iranians—whose president, Mahmood Ahmadinejad, has famously threatened to "wipe Israel off the map"—continued to defy international demands to abandon their nuclear ambitions.[33]

But if Israel is an obvious case, it is also an obvious exception. Despite brief periods of temptation in the United States in the 1950s and 1960s regarding the Soviet and Chinese nuclear programs, most nations only began to think seriously about prevention after the end of the Cold War. Israeli leaders, by contrast, long ago settled such questions for themselves, to some extent with the uneasy and unspoken approval of an international community, at least in the West, that recognized the unique and perilous situation of a tiny nation surrounded by enemy states with whom it is nearly constantly, in one way or another, at war.

Of course, the quiet acceptance of an Israeli exception is also to some extent a matter of self-interest on the part of Israel's friends and enemies alike. When the Israelis bombed the Iraqi nuclear program at Osirak in 1981, for example, there was public condemnation but implicit approval that the Iraqi situation had been defused, at least for the moment. No one, in the Middle East or anywhere else, really wanted to see Saddam Hussein gain a nuclear weapon. (One European defense official recalled later that the strike was greeted with "relief" at the time among many European defense ministries—even in Paris, despite the death of a French national in the raid and France's very public condemnation of the Israelis.)[34] The Americans, for their part, rebuked Israel at the United Nations and suspended a shipment of military aircraft, which was promptly resumed within months. Ten years later, U.S. defense secretary Dick Cheney would publicly thank the Israelis for the raid and for having "made our job easier" in the first Persian Gulf War against Iraq.[35]

Despite this toleration by at least some of the international community, however, the Israeli practice of prevention had little effect on international norms. Until the 1990s, most nations, including Israel's closest allies, condemned Israeli actions as unacceptable, even when they privately supported them. (Rochefoucauld was right: hypocrisy is indeed the tribute vice pays to virtue, especially in international affairs.) The norm against preventive action was honored by the international community even as it was accepted that at times the Israelis, among others, might have to breach it.

And yet, in the first years of the twenty-first century, more nations seem to be regarding prevention as increasingly acceptable and the norms against it as increasingly useless. The exception is in danger of becoming the rule. Despite the criticisms that have been leveled at the U.S. National Security Strategy since 2002, the question is not whether other countries have since been seeking to emulate the American example or replicate America's claims. The more pressing question is whether the rest of the world is, in effect, turning into Israel.

"We will strike. This includes preventive strikes."

Although international norms against preventive violence are eroding, they are not uniformly collapsing everywhere and in similar ways. Some nations are openly advocating and practicing prevention; others are more reluctantly accepting the possible use of preventive options, while others either are resisting or outright rejecting discretionary violence as a tool of national and international security.

Other than the United States and Israel, no nation has claimed a right to engage in preventive military action more insistently and more explicitly than the Russian Federation. But then, no major developed country—again with the exception of Israel—faces so many unpredictable threats within and around its borders. Critics would no doubt argue that Moscow's vicious conduct of its war against secessionists and Islamic extremists in Chechnya (who, it should be noted, are not always the same people), particularly under the leadership of Russian president Vladimir Putin, has virtually guaranteed that Russians would be the targets of terror. But whether the Russian government has given terrorists a pretext or not, terror attacks against the Russian Federation have been second only to 9/11 in their brutality and audacity. It is easy, especially for Americans, to forget that since the mid-1990s no nation has suffered more major terrorist incidents than Russia. The Americans by far have lost the most people in a single attack, and the unenviable record for small-scale attacks and suicide bombings has now, of course, passed from Israel to Iraq, which might be exempted from comparison as a special case, given that it is in the middle of a civil war. But the greatest number of mass-terror attacks have taken place in Russia.

These attacks have been marked by exceptional cruelty. In 1995, long before anyone outside St. Petersburg had heard of Vladimir Putin, Chechen raiders took an entire *hospital* hostage in a neighboring republic, a warning of the depths to which the terrorists were willing to sink. (Even the leader of the attack later lamented that his men "had turned into beasts" during the siege.)[36] More than 100 people eventually died in a botched rescue attempt. In 1999, a series of apartment buildings were bombed, although there are still claims that some of them were the work of the Russian secret services, and not Chechens.[37] In October 2002, Chechen terrorists, outfitted with explosive suicide belts, took over a theater in the heart of Moscow itself. More than 800 people were taken hostage, and scores died when Russian special forces gassed the building with anesthetic before raiding it. And in August 2004, two Russian airliners were simultaneously blown out of the sky by suicide bombers, killing nearly a hundred passengers and crew.

The following month brought the greatest outrage of all. In October

2004, a team of Chechens seized a school in the small town of Beslan. The attackers reportedly tortured the children, denied them food and water, forced them to drink their own urine, and raped some of the older girls.[38] Once again, a rescue attempt went wrong; nearly 800 people were wounded and more than 300 killed, including 186 children. The Russian people, horrified and in shock, wanted both revenge and protection at almost any price. Shortly after the massacre, pollsters found that 82 percent of Russians would "support actions aimed at destroying terrorists beyond Russia's borders" with two-thirds supporting "merging all of Russia's special services into a single organ resembling the Soviet-era KGB" in order to defend the country.[39]

Initially, however, Russian statements about prevention seemed directed more toward threats from other states, and perhaps even from the West, than from terrorists. A year before Beslan, the Russians made strikingly clear claims about prevention, both in a draft Russian defense doctrine published in October 2003 and in subsequent comments made by defense minister Sergei Ivanov, which were quickly dubbed the "Ivanov Doctrine" in the Western press. Ivanov declared that Russia could use preventive military force in cases where a threat is growing and is "visible, clear, and unavoidable." Moreover, such threats need not represent immediate and mortal peril; rather, Moscow reserved the right to engage in preventive action if "there is an attempt to limit Russia's access to regions that are essential to its survival, or those that are important from an economic or financial point of view."[40]

This caused a certain amount of consternation in the West, and Ivanov later tried to clarify the Russian position at a meeting in Colorado with NATO defense ministers. "The doctrine," he said, "does not specify any preventive nuclear strikes"—no doubt a relief to NATO and rogue states alike—"it merely implies that Russia retains the right to use military might for prevention, [former Soviet] countries included."[41] Reportedly, NATO ministers were told privately to ignore the Russian document, and Russian defense journalist Pavel Felgenhauer later suggested that the new doctrine was more a public relations maneuver in the midst of the 2004 Russian presidential campaign than an actual military doctrine—a questionable claim given that Putin had no real opposition and was in no danger of losing.[42] Moreover, a leading Russian military figure, president of the Russian Academy of Military Sciences General Makhmut Gareev, former deputy chief of the Soviet General Staff, claimed that the new talk of preemptive and preventive strikes was a major, even historical, shift in Russian doctrine. He attributed this change to the fact that "the nature of threats had radically shifted in the past decade" and that Russia had to be "ready to defend its interests and carry out allied commitments not only on its own territory but anywhere in the world."[43]

At the very least, the "Ivanov Doctrine" was probably meant to leave open the door for Russian action against sources of instability on its own borders, as Ivanov himself noted at the time in an interview with *Izvestiia*.[44] This makes sense not only in the context of ethnic and political clashes in the former Soviet sphere, but it also would reflect more recent Russian thinking on proliferation and instability. Veteran Russia watcher Dmitri Trenin wrote in early 2004:

> Whereas in Cold War days Moscow was obsessed with the U.S.-Soviet nuclear balance, the Russian Federation is paying more attention to the phenomenon of a weak yet nuclear-capable state: an unstable regime here, a divided country there, a local bully in another place, all of which enhance the chance of nuclear weapons actually being used. Positioned where it is, Russia has no interest in seeing more of its southern neighbors acquire nuclear arms.[45]

It is also possible that the Russian position in fact reflected anger over the Anglo-American attack on Iraq; at one point during the uproar over Ivanov's statement, President Putin affirmed that Russia "retains the right to launch a preemptive strike, *if this practice continues to be used around the world*" (emphasis added).[46] But the more likely explanation is that at the time Moscow was preparing a rationale for acting against what it saw as actual threats—or for imperial intervention, depending on one's point of view—primarily on its southern flanks.

In any case, there can be no question that Russia's experience with terrorism over the past decade has strongly affected Russian attitudes about prevention. A 2003 report by a group of Russian foreign policy experts, including some from the government, defined a new threat they labeled "megaterrorism," noting that this new, fantastically destructive, "cynical" terrorism has deep global systemic implications.[47] Russian defense analyst Andrei Piontkovksii has argued, like many of his American counterparts, that terrorists cannot be deterred or contained in the way those concepts have traditionally been applied, and therefore "can only be counteracted with preventive measures."[48] He also suggests that this is understood at the highest levels of the Russian leadership, despite hypocritical Russian condemnation of the Americans:

The declaration by the U.S., to the right to conduct preventive strikes as an intrinsic extension of the right of a nation to self-defense has been repeatedly criticized in the Russian press. Yet, here are . . . two quotes:

"If anyone tries to use weapons commensurate to weapons of mass destruction against our country, we will respond with measures adequate to the threat . . . at all locations . . . I underline, no matter where they are."

"In such cases, and I officially confirm this, we will strike. This includes preventive strikes."

"Who are these hawks," he asks, "preaching a concept of preventive strikes violating the sacred principle of national state sovereignty? Donald Rumsfeld, Paul Wolfowitz, Dick Cheney, Condoleezza Rice?"[49] In fact, as Piontkovskii pointed out, they are from statements by President Putin and Defense Minister Ivanov.

After the Beslan tragedy, Russian officials became even more strident in asserting a right to preventive action. Colonel General Yurii Baluyevski, chief of the Russian General Staff, declared in September 2004: "As for carrying out preventive strikes against terrorist bases . . . we will take all measures to liquidate terrorist bases in any region of the world." This produced a rather nervous reaction from European Union officials, who felt the need to reaffirm EU objections to "extra-judicial killings."[50] A few days later, Putin himself warned that Russia was "seriously preparing to act preventively against terrorists."[51]

Russian diplomatic and military officials have since continued to insist that Russia strongly opposes unilateral actions without UN sanction.[52] However, Moscow's position also takes advantage of legal innovations regarding preemption, and leaves plenty of room for discretionary action, particularly against terrorists, as an official 2005 statement from the Russian Foreign Ministry made clear:

The law [of self defense] *in its modern understanding* in light of new threats to international and national security absolutely includes the right to self-defense in the event of a mass-scale terrorist attack on the state . . . . In the case where a nation has been subjected to a terrorist attack and has serious reason to suppose that a repeat of that attack from an established source is inevitable, the government, in the course of realizing its right to self-defense, may take the necessary measures to liquidate or mitigate such a gathering threat. (emphasis added)[53]

Thus, while the Russian position seems to be rooted in a firm opposition to preventive strikes (at least by any nation besides Russia) without proper international permission, this absolutism is hard to square with numerous statements about what Russia believes are its rights regarding terrorists and other threats, especially in neighboring former Soviet states.

Russian security and military documents, like their Soviet predecessors, are often more statements of political intent than actual plans of action, and it is possible that the uncompromising language in the Ivanov Doctrine and other Russian declarations is mostly a reflection of the trauma of over a decade of ghastly terror attacks. But other nations, while less strident, are showing no less interest in similar solutions to seemingly intractable security problems.

The Reluctant Preventionists

Among America's European allies, Great Britain has been the most enthusiastic supporter of the kind of preventive thinking that led the United States to seek war in Iraq. The sense of danger among some British leaders is acute. Home Secretary John Reid said in mid-2006 that the United Kingdom is "probably in the most sustained period of severe threat since the end of World War II," a remarkable and revealing statement given that Britain and its NATO bases were squarely in the Soviet nuclear crosshairs during the Cold War.[54] The real question is how deep this commitment to prevention goes in London, as it is closely associated with Prime Minister Tony Blair, much as prevention in the United States, particularly after Iraq, is identified with President Bush. But just as the problem of prevention will likely outlive the Bush administration, so too will the same questions bedevil British governments long after Blair's exit.

What marks the British approach to prevention, as in Europe overall, is a kind of reluctance that is missing from the more muscular American and Russian versions. Blair, to be sure, is firm in his defense of preventive military action, but in 2003 he made it clear as well that he felt it was a conclusion he was forced to reach because the nature of the enemy:

I tell you honestly what my fear is, my fear is that we wake up one day and we find either that one of these dictatorial states has used weapons of mass destruction—and Iraq has done so in the past—and we get sucked into a conflict, with all the devastation that would cause; or alternatively these weapons, which are being traded right round the world at the moment, fall into the hands of these terrorist groups, these fanatics who will stop at absolutely nothing to cause death and destruction on a mass scale. Now that is what I have to worry about. And I understand of course why people think it is a very remote threat and it is far away and why does it bother us. Now I simply say to you, it is a matter of time unless we act and take a stand before terrorism and weapons of mass destruction come together, and I regard them as two sides of the same coin.[55]

Blair linked this argument to previous thinking about humanitarian interventions, and argued that preventive action against dangerous rogues like Iraq is both required by the demands of national security and justifiable as a service to mankind. "Emphatically I am not saying that every situation leads to military action. But we surely have a duty and a right to prevent the threat materializing; and we surely have a responsibility to act when a nation's people are subjected to a regime such as Saddam's."[56]

Again, whether Blair's fellow Britons will continue to agree with his preventive stance after his departure from Downing Street is unclear. The July 2005 bombing of the London transportation system by British Islamists boosted Blair's approval rating at the time, and subsequent polls, according to *London Times* U.S. editor Gerard Baker,

showed large majorities in favor of keeping British troops in Iraq and, most strikingly, a jump in the number of Brits who believed their country should stay close to the United States in its foreign policy—now a clear majority—rather than striking out on its own or siding with the Europeans. . . . The mood in the House of Commons [shortly after the attacks] reflected the mood in the nation. Even Tony Blair's critics seemed captured by a new sobriety in the face of this threat and pledged their support for him.[57]

Yet British citizens, like their American counterparts, are fed up with the morass in Iraq, and do not seem inclined to further preventive adventures. They definitely no longer share Blair's opinion of George W. Bush: a November 2006 poll found that a majority of the British thought that Bush was a more dangerous leader than Kim Jong Il.[58] (President Bush could at least take consolation that Osama bin Laden still took top honors in the UK as the most dangerous person in the world.)

It is unlikely that Britain's Labor or Conservative party will produce another leader who is as forceful, and eloquent, a defender of prevention as Tony Blair. (The Liberal Democrats were staunch opponents of the Iraq invasion and are even less likely to embrace any notions of prevention.) But this does not mean that British thinking about national security will necessarily undergo a dramatic shift with Blair gone, not least because Blair's policies are not as far outside the European main-stream as they might appear at first blush. As Tomas Valasek wrote in 2003, "Britain's position . . . is clear: it has stood alongside the United States throughout Washington's campaign to disarm Iraq, by force if necessary. But Britain is not alone."[59]

France is perhaps the most prominent example of a European power that is gradually, if reluctantly, coming to grips with the problem of prevention, an especially interesting trend given the unswerving opposition of the Chirac government to the war in Iraq. In 2002, the Defense Ministry released its "2003–2008 Military Program" in Paris at about the same time the U.S. National Security Strategy was being released in Washington. In it the French minister of defense noted that while France now enjoys the protection to its east of a stable and peaceful Europe, this new strategic depth did little to protect France against new and "unusual and unexpected" conflicts, including "multiple and often asymmetrical threats" from "state or non-state entities . . . looking to bypass our defenses and take advantage of our weaknesses by any means possible, including non-military."[60]

The French analysis then notes that this danger took on special significance after 9/11:

Through the scale of their violence and the number of victims, the period beginning with the 11 September 2001 attacks have sanctioned the emergence of mass terrorism. These attacks have opened the way to different types of conflicts, without battlefields and without clearly defined armies, where the enemy, ready to use weapons of mass destruction, clearly aims at civilian populations.

This in itself is not remarkable, as it merely acknowledges the reality of the post-9/11 world. What is noteworthy, however, is the proposed response to this environment, and it is worth quoting at length:

On this basis, in today's context of foreseeable risks and threats, we must pay greater attention to missions of protection and to the means that allow the prevention or foiling of aggression within the framework of prevention and projection. Nuclear deterrence is still our fundamental guarantee. At the same time, general military strategy consists of prevention, protection, and projection-action in order to address other kinds of threats with the necessary flexibility. . . . Outside our borders, within the framework of prevention and projection-action [sic], we must be able to identify and prevent threats as soon as possible.

Within this framework, possible preemptive action is not out of the question, where an explicit and confirmed threat has been recognized. This determination and the improvement of long range strike should constitute a deterrent threat for our potential aggressors, especially as transnational terrorist networks develop and organize outside our territory, in areas not governed by states, and even at times with the help of enemy states. . . . Prevention is the first step in the implementation of our defense strategy, for which the options are grounded in the appearance of the asymmetric threat phenomenon.

This embrace of prevention was so direct, at least in the eyes of some observers, that the French government quickly had to deny charges that it had abandoned nuclear deterrence in favor of preemptive nuclear strikes against rogue nuclear arsenals.[61]

To some extent, alarm about the French use of the term "prevention" was misplaced, since the word, in the French context, also includes so-called "soft" prevention, the use of diplomacy and other means to "prevent" threats. As French diplomat Philippe Errera, the deputy director for disarmament and nuclear nonproliferation at the Quai d'Orsay, has put it, the difference between the French and American conception of soft prevention is that the French actually take the idea seriously as a possible solution.[62] Errera admits the possibility of unilateral military action, but he chides the Americans primarily for stating as a "doctrine" what used to be only one option among many. But the French document, as one of its drafters later confirmed, was explicitly meant to include military action if all else fails.[63]

The French security strategy was symbolically dated September 11, 2002, which might seem to make it little more than the French government's reaction to both the events of 9/11 and the subsequent U.S. National Security Strategy. But the actual document was drafted two years before 9/11, and an early version, with language almost identical to the final legislation, was submitted to the previous Socialist government in early 2001.[64] Heisbourg notes that prevention can be found in French thinking as early as the French Ministry of Defense white paper of 1994, but even in 1981, as Gilles Andréani recalls, outgoing French president Valéry Giscard d'Estaing briefed successor François Mitterrand on three important issues in French security policy: a matter that is apparently still classified, the general status of France's nuclear forces, and a plan for the preventive removal of Libya's Moammar Khaddafy on the grounds that he had become an intolerable danger.[65]

In the end, as the saying goes, actions speak louder than words. While the 2003 war against Iraq reduced Franco-American relations to a chilliness not seen since France withdrew from NATO's military command in

1966, it did not mean that France, Europe, and the United States no longer agreed on a common threat. France continues to host Alliance Base, a multinational intelligence center in Paris where French, American, British, Canadian, German, and Australian operatives gather not only to share intelligence but to conduct actual, and strictly secret, operations. The organization, whose working language is French, is headed by a French general and claims to have broken at least a dozen major cases and made numerous arrests.[66]

In way, it is disingenuous to speak of a "European" approach to prevention; as Errera has noted, the "European" debate is really more of a negotiation between British, French, and to some extent Russian views on security matters.[67] Smaller nations in Europe do not have the political or military clout to alter norms regarding the use of force. (Germany, of course, is a special case when considering the use of force, but even the Germans have shown a renewed interest, as Kosovo demonstrated, in participating in maintaining international order.) The European Union itself, however, has taken up the question of the defense of the Continent as a whole, and its conclusions, while more tentative, are not dramatically different from French, British, or even Russian thinking on the subject of prevention.

The European Union released its Basic Principles for an EU Strategy Against Proliferation of Weapons of Mass Destruction in June 2003, even as its members were split over the war in Iraq only weeks earlier, and then issued a more general "European Security Strategy" six months later. The Basic Principles understandably echoed the anxieties expressed by the American, British, and other members of the "coalition of the willing" in the approach to war, but also reflected the discord among EU members about the use of force against would-be proliferators.[68] Still, in an insightful comment, the report acknowledged that weapons of mass destruction "are different from other weapons not only because of their capacity to cause death on a large scale but also because they could destabilize the international system."[69] Moreover, the

acquisition of WMD or related materials by terrorists would represent an additional threat to the international system with potentially uncontrollable consequences. Armed with weapons or materials of mass destruction terrorists could inflict damage that in the past only states with large armies could achieve.

And while the EU document argues for early multilateral political and diplomatic solutions to such threats, in the end it allows for forcible disarmament—or, in other words, prevention: "When these measures (including political dialogue and diplomatic pressure) have failed, coercive measures under Chapter VII of the UN Charter and international law (sanctions, selective or global, interceptions of shipments and, as appropriate, the use of force) could be envisioned."

The EU Security Strategy released in December 2003 was an even bolder document. Titled "A Secure Europe in a Better World," it included unmistakable references to preventive measures. British scholar Anne Deighton has argued that the EU attempt to create a security strategy was in part driven by the unveiling of the 2002 U.S. National Security Strategy; its

articulation of the chilling shift to national preemption if [America's] own interests were threatened was a spur to the EU to devise some form of collective, if indirect European response. The December 2003 European Security Strategy document was then not so much a formal strategy as the term is conventionally understood, but rather a form of sticking plaster for the EU Member States to help cover their own differences, to find common ground, and to draw up a joint credo with which it could both collectively respond to the Bush administration's policies, and build upon the developments of the past four years in the [European] foreign policy . . . sphere.[70]

Deighton's point is well taken, but the European strategy was more than merely a reaction to the Bush NSS and the invasion of Iraq. This is especially evident given that the language of the EU strategy shows the same kind of concerns voiced in Moscow, Washington, and Paris even before the American NSS was released in 2002. It recognizes that "with . . . new threats, the first line of defense will often be abroad," a passage that one of the strategy's drafters, Robert Cooper (EU Director-General for External and Politico-Military Affairs and top advisor to EU foreign policy chief Javier Solana) has affirmed was meant explicitly to include the possibility of preventive military action.[71]

In any case, transatlantic differences of opinion over security are not particularly pronounced, despite the short rift between Europeans (or at least some Europeans) and Americans (or at least some Americans) over the war in Iraq. Each year, the German Marshall Fund conducts polling in the United States and various European nations about major questions of foreign policy, and the results over the past five years suggest a broader agreement on threats, and what to do about them, than might otherwise be expected. There is a strong and continuing Atlantic consensus, for example, on the most important menaces to international order, with Islamic fundamentalism, terrorism, and WMD proliferation predictably topping the list. In some areas, Europeans are just as willing to use force as their American friends, and in a few cases, even more so. Majorities polled in 2004 in the U.S. and Europe would be "willing to use military force to remove a government that abuses human rights," with more Europeans, but a minority of Americans, willing to "use force to stop a civil war." And when asked whether "military action to eliminate terrorist organizations is the most appropriate way to fight terrorism," clear majorities in the U.S., France, Great Britain, the Netherlands, Poland, Portugal, and Turkey agreed, with pluralities of at least 40 percent in Germany, Italy, and Spain also agreeing.[72]

Perhaps more revealing were answers to a question that goes to the heart of the prevention problem. When asked, a year after the invasion of Iraq, if their country should use armed force—with United Nations approval—"to intervene in a foreign country to eliminate the threat of a terrorist attack," majorities, often of two-thirds or more, in the United States and every EU nation surveyed agreed, with France leading at 82 percent. (Turkey was the sole exception.) NATO approval was not quite as important, with most respondents by a very small margin preferring UN permission to NATO authorization. But that margin in the UN's favor was small indeed, with most people in the U.S. and Europe just as willing to take military action with the approval of their closest allies as with that of the UN or NATO. This trend was especially pronounced in the United States: as the Marshall study noted, for "Americans, the approval of the main European allies provides a higher degree of legitimacy for the use of military force than the approval of either the UN or NATO."

However, there are limits to the perceived value of the United Nations even in Europe. When asked whether "it is justified to bypass the United Nations when the vital interests of your country are involved," majorities in the United States, the United Kingdom, the Netherlands, and Slovakia agreed, as did significant pluralities in France, Germany, Poland, and Portugal. From 2003 to 2004, despite the war in Iraq, support for bypassing the UN actually *increased* in France, Germany, the Netherlands, Poland, and Portugal. Nor was this an aberration; the same question, when asked in 2005, again showed slight increases in agreement in the U.S., France, Germany, the UK, Italy, the Netherlands, Portugal, and Spain. (For some reason, the question was not asked again in 2006.)

In the end, both Americans and Europeans are willing to use force to protect their national security from even potential threats, with or without the United Nations. This is a finding that not only indicates the rising temptation of prevention but also provides some grounds for the worst fears of those who believe the great powers might become increasingly unwilling to seek international permission before using their considerable military might. America, Russia, and Europe see similar threats and are reaching similar conclusions about how to deal with them. Ironically, the United States and the Russian Federation, former enemies though they were, are perhaps most alike in their approach to prevention. One major difference between them, of course, is that the U.S. actually has the ability to project its power in ways the Russians can only envy, but that doesn't change the fact that there is substantial conceptual agreement between the former superpowers about prevention. By contrast, the Europeans, with the British and the French in the lead, are reluctantly but surely finding their way toward a new understanding of the use of force in what they see as a more dangerous and unpredictable world.

Pacific Anxieties

It could be argued that Europe, with its large Muslim population, its experience with major terror plots, and its physical proximity to the Middle East and Central Asia, would naturally gravitate toward preventive options. There is nothing to recommend prevention to political leaders more convincingly than a failure to avert a terrorist attack, as changing attitudes in the United States and Europe attest. But these are not anxieties limited to the western hemisphere.

In 2002—a year before Australia would commit its military forces to the invasion of Iraq—an Islamic extremist group associated with al-Qaeda bombed a nightclub in Bali, Indonesia frequented by Western tourists. The attack killed more than 200 people, most of them Westerners. Nearly half of those killed were Australians, and the bombing created a sense of vulnerability and deep anger in Australia. Why the Islamists would needlessly pick a fight with the Australians is one of the many imponderables of the confused state of terrorist strategy, but Australian leaders were not cowed by the Bali attack and instead have since argued for going on the offensive against terrorists.

A month after the Bali bombing, Australian defense minister Robert

Hill gave a seminal speech at the University of Adelaide in which he discussed how Australia was wrestling with changes in the international security environment. Noting that "the circumstances of the post cold war environment are testing the international framework," Hill questioned whether previous understandings about the use of force had now become outdated.

> Australia has consistently affirmed that any actions that are taken by this country will be consistent with international law. The question to be asked, however, is whether international law has kept pace with the changed circumstances that have evolved in the world since the end of the cold war as it relates to today's conflicts—crimes against humanity, genocide, religious ethnic and communal conflicts, global terrorism and the like.[73]

Hill then discussed the venerable *Caroline* test, and called for a reinterpretation of its central principles of imminence and necessity. "How should these principles be interpreted," he asked, "in the age of over-the-horizon weaponry, computer network attack and asymmetric threats when warning times are reduced virtually to zero and enemies can strike almost anywhere?"

Hill claimed only to have questions, not answers, but there can be little doubt where he was heading with his criticism of the *Caroline* standard.

> It is clear that, when an armed attack against a State is imminent, that State is not compelled to wait until the first blow has been struck. But what action can a State legitimately take when that attack is to be launched by a non-State actor, in a non-conventional manner, operating from a variety of bases in disparate parts of the world? There are no tell-tale warning indicators such as the mobilization and pre-deployment of conventional forces.

While Hill declined to side openly with those who "would argue that it's time for a new and distinct doctrine of preemptive action," he nonetheless in the next breath called on "the international community and the international lawyers to seek an agreement on the ambit of the right to self defense better suited to contemporary realities." There was an implied threat as well that those lawyers had best get to work quickly, because in the "meantime those responsible for governance will continue to interpret self-defense as necessary to protect their peoples and their nations' interests."

A few days later, Australian prime minister John Howard gave an interview to journalist Laurie Oakes. Like his defense minister, Howard suggested that both the UN Charter and international law itself needed to be changed to allow more flexibility in attacking terrorists. Oakes broached the subject of discretionary action with Howard directly: "Now, you've been arguing for a new approach to pre-emptive defence, you want the UN to change its charter, I think. Does that mean that you . . . if you knew that, say, JI people [Jemaah Islamiya, the group that bombed the Bali nightclub] in another neighbouring country were planning an attack on Australia that you would be prepared to act?" Howard responded:

Oh yes, I think any Australian Prime Minister would. I mean, it stands to reason that if you believed that somebody was going to launch an attack against your country, either of a conventional kind or of a terrorist kind, and you had a capacity to stop it and there was no alternative other than to use that capacity then of course you would have to use it.[74]

Oakes pressed Howard further. "It's fair to say, isn't it, that the SAS [Australian special forces] is not only perfectly tailored to make that kind of pre-emptive strike in another country but that's really what we've got it for." Howard, while not explicitly committing himself to a policy of prevention, left little doubt about how he would react to such a threat: "Laurie, there's no situation that I'm aware of at the moment that raises that issue, and I don't really want to go down that path any further other than to state the obvious that any Prime Minister who had a capacity to prevent an attack against his country would be failing the most basic test of office if he didn't utilise that capacity if there's no other alternative."

As with George Bush and Tony Blair, it is possible that this rethinking of Australian security policy will last only as long as the Howard government. But Howard has been following public opinion as much as leading it, and, as Australian writer Gerard Henderson has pointed out, "for the foreseeable future" among "the majority of Australians" there will be "ongoing majority support for the war against terrorism in its various formats."[75] Henderson also raised the question of whether different leaders would reach different conclusions in such a threatening environment: "No democratically elected leader in the U.S., Britain or Australia wants a situation to emerge whereby they could have prevented a weapon of mass destruction getting into the hands of a terrorist group but failed to act."[76] Howard, for his part, was reelected handily in 2004, despite his close relationship with George Bush and his commitment of Australian troops to the invasion of Iraq.

In a sense, Australia's call for changes in international norms about the use of force should not be all that unexpected. It is surrounded by several potentially unstable regimes and, after Bali, is facing an obvious threat from Islamists. (In 2005, Australian police broke up a plot by a group of Muslims that they believed was aimed at targets in Sydney, including a possible rocket attack on a nuclear reactor near the city.)[77] With one of the most effective military forces in the region, Australia can expect to be called upon not only to take preventive measures to ensure its own security, but at times to establish stability in the region, as it did with over 5000 troops in East Timor in 1999. Although the Timor operation was approved by the United Nations, the Australian government, like others, is clearly looking ahead to situations in which threats are less obvious and UN approval less likely or even impossible.

Australian thinking on preemption and prevention is largely being shaped by the threat of terrorism. But that debate has not taken on the sharpness or urgency that is sometimes found in the United States and Europe, for various reasons: Australia has not yet been threatened by mass-scale terror, it does not face an existential threat to its existence, and it is generally on good terms with its neighbors (and for that matter, with most of the world).

If only Japan were so fortunate.

Part of the price Japan paid for its imperial aggression against its neighbors in the first half of the twentieth century was to live under a "peace constitution" dictated by the victors of World War II that capped the size of the Japanese military and committed Japan's armed forces to purely defensive missions. As a reformed democracy and an American ally, Japan enjoyed the protection of American military power, but that protection also cost the Japanese a certain amount of control over their ability to shape their own defense and security policies. During the Cold War, this was an arrangement that served both Japanese and American purposes: the United States needed Japanese bases to protect its Pacific flank from China and the Soviet Union, and Japan needed some form of military security that would not alarm its neighbors.

But with the Soviet Union gone and Japan's only avowed enemy, North Korea, finally a proven nuclear power, the Japanese are now in the midst of the most heated and important debate over their national security since 1945. There is even discussion about whether Japan—the only country in the world ever to suffer atomic attack—should itself possess nuclear weapons. Reckless North Korean policies, including numerous missile tests over the past decade and, finally, the successful explosion of a nuclear device in 2006, have helped overcome Japanese reticence about previously taboo possibilities. "The Japanese people are very angry and very worried," Japanese professor Tetsuo Maeda said after a series of unsuccessful but threatening North Korean missile tests in July 2006, "and, right now, they will accept any government plan for the military."[78] While the Japanese government at this writing has reached no firm conclusion on any such plans, prevention is figuring prominently in debates in Tokyo.

Although North Korea's 2006 "missiles of July" added considerable fuel to these debates, the regime's continuous and somewhat unhinged threats helped to bolster the case of Japanese alarmists and to bring the previously muted Japanese debate over prevention into the open even before yet another of Kim Jong Il's failed experiments in ballistics corkscrewed into the Sea of Japan. In early 2003 the head of the Japan Defense Agency, Shigeru Ishiba, was asked by a Japanese legislator what the government would do in the event North Korea declared it would, yet again, "turn Tokyo into a sea of fire" and then began clear preparations to launch ballistic missiles. Ishiba replied: "If North Korea expresses the intention of turning Tokyo into a sea of fire and if it begins preparations [to attack], for instance by fueling [its missiles], we will consider [North Korea] is initiating [a military attack]."[79] Foreign Minister Yoriko Kawaguchi, present at the same meeting, agreed. Ishiba later stressed that, even with Japan's Peace Constitution, "just to be on the receiving end of the attack is not what our constitution had in mind. . . . Just to wait for another country's attack and lose thousands and tens of thousands of people, that is not what the constitution assumes."[80] Ishiba reiterated this point a month after his initial comments, saying that it would be too late to act if North Korean missiles were already on their way, and that preemption would be "a self-defense measure" if North Korea were to "resort to arms against Japan."[81]

Tokyo later backpedaled somewhat, and announced that in the event of a North Korean missile strike the government would meet, "inspect the damage, consult the United States, and denounce North Korea," and Ishiba himself clarified his earlier statements Japan would not use its own forces against the North, but would rely on U.S. forces to strike back in the event of hostilities.[82] Despite these "clarifications," debate continued at the highest levels in Japan. As foreign policy analyst Rajan Menon wrote in 2003:

Proponents of jettisoning military minimalism are to be found both within the [Japanese] government and in academic circles. They have called for removing constitutional restraints on the acquisition and use of military power, building weapons that extend the reach of the [Japan Self Defense Forces] (aircraft that can refuel in flight and aircraft carriers, for instance), erecting a national missile defense system, even acquiring nuclear arms and the capability to eliminate nuclear threats with pre-emptive strikes.

More important, Menon points out that advocates of such initiatives "are no longer considered extremists or militarists and, in some cases, include senior officials who, in earlier times, would have been fired for their lack of caution."[83]

Not only were such officials not fired, but one was even elected prime minister in 2006. Shinzo Abe has been a consistent advocate of redefining Japan's defense posture; shortly after the North Korean missile launches (and two months before his election as Japan's leader), he said: "If we accept that there is no other option to prevent an attack . . . there is the view that that attacking the launch base of the guided missiles is within the constitutional right of self-defense."[84] Foreign Minister Taro Aso, whom Abe would keep on in his cabinet, took a similar line, arguing that "when missiles are being targeted at Japan, we cannot just stand by and wait to get hit."[85]

The Japanese, however, are hardly unanimous in supporting statements like these. In addition to public protests and editorial-page objections, other Japanese politicians, including those from Abe's own party, have opposed tough talk about preemption and first strikes. Taku Yamasaki, a senior member of the ruling Liberal Democratic Party, said he was "taken aback" and "couldn't believe my ears" when listening to younger LDP members discussing first-strike options against North Korea. "The whole LDP," Yamasaki said during the missile crisis with the North Koreans, "seems to have forgotten [its] basic post-war security [policy]" of defensive pacifism.[86] Another LDP leader expressed surprise at Abe's remarks in particular, and doubted whether they reflected any real change in Japanese policy. "While it is easy to say 'let's hit enemy bases' or 'let's possess such capability and weapons'," former LDP chief Koichi Kato chided, "officials should not say such things."[87] Perhaps most telling is that there is no evidence yet that Tokyo is spending the money to reconfigure its forces for more aggressive or proactive missions.[88]

But the fact that the Japanese are openly discussing preemption and prevention is a sign of a significant change in thinking in Tokyo, including among government leaders. Like the short-lived attraction to preventive war in America in the 1950s, it is not a debate limited to the fringe or to extremists. Whether prevention is discarded as quickly in Japan in the early twenty-first century as it was in the United States in the mid-twentieth century is difficult to say, since the comparison is somewhat inexact. The Americans, faced with a Soviet Union that was too strong to overwhelm—and that sought, however cynically, some form of dialogue with its enemies in Washington—chose to forgo igniting a massive and destructive world war. North Korea, with its outrageous threats, its rather strange leader, and its small arsenal (whose size and vulnerability are themselves temptations to prevention) might prove to be a more lasting spur to the prevention debate in Japan, at least as long as it ruled by a reclusive and unpredictable totalitarian.

The Chinese Dilemma

Nothing could be more indicative of a coming age of preventive violence than the fact that four of the five permanent members of the United Nations Security Council, the group charged with keeping the peace in the international commons, have adopted some form of prevention in their national security policies. Not coincidentally, all four are industrialized democracies—Russia, at least so far, still counts as a democracy, however illiberal it may have turned under Vladimir Putin—and all face significant threats both from terrorists and from rogue nuclear proliferators.

This would seem to leave the People's Republic of China, the world's largest authoritarian state, as the sole dissenter on the question of prevention. The Chinese, however, find themselves in an unusual situation, and their opposition to preventive action, while rhetorically firm, is actually somewhat more complicated than it appears.

Authoritarian states can be counted on to be the most ardent enemies of prevention, primarily because they know full well that they are likely to be its most obvious targets.[89] Dictatorships naturally wish to abuse the rights of their citizens without the annoying interference of the rest of the international community, and to this end they strenuously defend the traditional Westphalian understanding of absolute sovereignty. In its day, the Soviet Union was a consistent champion of the strictest observance of the inviolability of the rights of sovereign states—except, of course, when Moscow was busy violating the rights of the sovereign states in its orbit. (The Soviet approach to sovereignty could be termed the "Animal House" rule. When two fraternity brothers in the 1978 film saw the campus bully hazing one of their initiates, they were indignant: "Hey, *they* can't do that to our pledges . . . only *we* can do that to our pledges!") Much the same could be said of the Americans, but the USSR and other authoritarian states were acutely aware of their vulnerabilities as dictatorships, and this made international cooperation on a variety of issues, such as human rights or journalistic freedom, particularly difficult.

China is no exception. Beijing, like its smaller authoritarian friends around the world, has long insisted that the international community adhere to scrupulous norms of non-interference in the affairs of other states. This is to be expected from a country that crushes dissent, oppresses various religious and ethnic groups, and maintains a chain of slave labor camps. But the Chinese aspire as well to something like legitimacy as a respected member of the international community, and so the Chinese approach has been to allow, but not to support or oppose, certain kinds of intervention. The Chinese government, as American scholar Denny Roy has put it, "has consistently demonstrated a desire to cultivate a responsible and prestigious international image and to be consulted on important international issues."[90] Rather than exercise the raw power of the veto in the Security Council and thus appear obstructionist, China has increasingly mastered the more subtle art of the abstention.

There are many examples of this conflicted Chinese behavior. In 1990, Beijing did not oppose (but again, did not support) the resolutions that led to the first Gulf War with Saddam Hussein, because, as Roy noted, it "would have been politically costly for China to oppose a policy that commanded a large degree of international support."[91] As Yan Xuetong, director of the Institute of International Studies at China's Qinghua University, put it at the time, "We don't want to stand alone."[92] China, whatever its policies at home, is not a rogue state and has no wish to be perceived as one, or as defending one, by an international community from whom it seeks legitimacy and respect.

Beijing took a similar stance in the 1994 debate over UN Security Council Resolution 940, which authorized action to create a multinational (read: U.S.) force to restore the elected government of Haiti to power. The resolution caused concern among some Latin American nations, particularly Brazil, as the Security Council was in fact authorizing U.S. military action in the Americas. But Brazil, of course, does not have a veto. China, had it chosen to quash the resolution, would have found itself at odds with the other four permanent members of the Council, and so Beijing in the end joined Brazil in abstaining. Restoring someone like Haitian president Jean-Bertrand Aristide to office may not, in the long run, have been all that palatable a choice, but China chose in any case to stand aside rather than press a theoretical point about Haitian sovereignty.

The contours of China's position on intervention became clearer in the debate over attacking Serbia in 1999, even though the matter never made it to the Security Council. Beijing strongly opposed NATO military action over Kosovo on three related grounds: that foreign forces had entered a domestic dispute, that NATO had bypassed the UN, and that military force had been used to NATO's ends.[93] But that does not mean that China is uniformly opposed to intervention: Chinese scholar Chu Shulong has argued that issue is not intervention itself, but rather its context. "Many of the differences dividing Asians, and especially the Chinese, from the rest of the world go beyond this or that case of intervention. The real difference lies in the conditions and processes of intentional interventions."[94] In other words, under strictly defined circumstances, including a clear threat to international order as Chapter VII of the UN Charter demands—and with UN approval an inflexible condition—the People's Republic might countenance certain actions in practice even while disapproving of them in principle. Kosovo, in the Chinese view, flunked both of these central tests.

The 9/11 attacks were both a problem and an opportunity for Beijing. On the one hand, there was no credible way that China, as a leader in the United Nations and in the international community more broadly, could even think of standing in the way of international action against the Taliban in the wake of the global horror at the massacres in New York and Washington. "Had China taken a neutral or unsupportive stance in the antiterrorism campaign," Roy notes, "many foreign observers would have questioned China's good international citizenship."[95] On the other hand, a country that continues to define America as its primary enemy in the world could not be comfortable with endorsing U.S. military action.

But Chinese leaders cannily realized as well that there could be significant benefits in supporting a generic "war on terror," particularly since the central government in Beijing was itself trying to snuff out an Uighur separatist movement in western China.[96] To some extent, the queasiness about allowing an attack on a sovereign state was elided by the fact that only Pakistan, the United Arab Emirates, and Saudi Arabia recognized the Taliban as the government of Afghanistan. And the Chinese, like the Russians in their war with the Chechens, no doubt hoped for some insulation from charges of human rights violations if they appeared cooperative in a common fight against terrorism. Beijing gambled—in vain, as it turned out—that in return for Chinese support for Operation Enduring Freedom, the Americans would sign off on equating the separatist Uighurs with the mass murderers of al-Qaeda, an equivalence the Americans have since shown no sign of accepting.[97]

Interestingly, the Chinese made no serious attempts to head off war between the U.S. and Iraq in 2003. Indeed, a September 2002 editorial in one of China's official newspapers warned Baghdad about "the last chance for Saddam Hussein to deprive the Americans of a legal case against himself," and China two months later voted for Security Council Resolution 1441, which was intended, however unsuccessfully, as a last warning of impending but unspecified "serious consequences" should Saddam fail to cooperate.[98] The Chinese may have thought it imprudent, or even unjustified, to go to war to depose Saddam Hussein, but in the end they chose not to prevent it.

Chinese patience seems to be running out with Kim Jong Il as well. According to former Chinese foreign ministry official Anne Wu in 2005, Beijing has been distancing itself from the North Korean regime, warning it that its support is not unqualified, not least due to Chinese fears that reckless North Korean behavior will spark an Asian arms race that could leave China surrounded by new nuclear powers, including Taiwan and South Korea.[99]

Still, China is no friend of prevention. Like other autocratic regimes, China's rulers have a vested interest in saving as much of the bygone Westphalian order as they can salvage. But the question remains whether China can continue to insist on a standard of sovereignty that a growing number of countries—including all its permanent colleagues on the Security Council—increasingly reject.

On to Baghdad

Even if an international consensus—or at least a consensus among the more powerful members of the international community—is forming regarding a more permissive standard regarding prevention, the question remains whether that consensus will survive the consequences of the invasion and occupation of Iraq. Even those sympathetic to arguments in favor of preventive action, like the European Union's Robert Cooper, now note that the concept of prevention "has 'Iraq' written all over it" due to America's clumsy handling of the war.[100] No weapons of mass destruction were found, no nuclear materials were recovered, and the world reacted with disgust as an illicit video recorded how Saddam Hussein was crudely taunted during his last minutes on the gallows. Given the failure of the preventive war launched as Operation Iraqi Freedom actually to *prevent* anything, will the gathering momentum toward prevention be dispersed by the realization, too often forgotten, that war is a costly and risky business?

Chapter 5

After Iraq

> *People who opposed this war feel vindicated and will feel even stronger about the risks of the doctrine of preventive war.*
>
> —*Jens Van Scherpenberg, German Institute for International and Security Affairs, 2004*

> *One of the most remarkable features of the Iraq war is that it did not discredit the argument that preventive war must remain "on the table" as a way of preventing the proliferation of weapons of mass destruction.*
>
> —*David Hendrickson and Robert Tucker, 2006*

Giving Prevention a "Bad Name"?

There is a certain irony in discussing the influence of Operation Iraqi Freedom (OIF), the 2003 invasion of Iraq, on norms and perceptions regarding preventive war. Philippe Errera captured the sentiments of many observers of the war and its aftermath in 2006 when he noted that one of the "profound effects" of the war was that it had "given prevention a bad name."[1] It is hard to imagine that prevention could have a worse name than it already had over the past three centuries, but OIF is something of a special case. Other than the actual execution of military operations against the various forces encountered during the initial Anglo-American invasion, the performance of the U.S.-led coalition has since been plagued by errors, miscalculations, bureaucratic tangles, and an overall atmosphere of incompetence made even more infuriating by the arrogant stubbornness of an administration that has taken more than three years to admit any of its mistakes in the postwar occupation. To take but one example, Coalition Provisional Authority head L. Paul Bremer was still insisting as late as 2006 that disbanding the Iraqi army— perhaps one of the greatest blunders in the first days of victory—was in fact the single smartest thing the Americans did after the war, an assertion that would be laughable were it not so tragically wrong.[2] As of this writing, more than 3,500 American soldiers have lost their lives, with many thousands more wounded.

And so Operation Iraqi Freedom is increasingly viewed, in the United States and around the world, as a sin twice compounded: not only was it a preventive war, but it now seems to have been an unnecessary war as well, as there was no gathering threat that needed to be prevented (or to use the White House's term, preempted) in the first place. No weapons of mass destruction, the nominal cause of the war, were found, a particularly embarrassing problem since the Bush administration, as one account later recalled, "incoherently [made] several competing cases for removing Saddam Hussein . . . finally settling on UN resolutions concerning WMD as the one cause it could best sell both at home and abroad as justification for the war."[3] But in a matter of a year or so, none of these many justifications mattered, and the American people turned against the war in Iraq in several ways. Since 2004, a majority continue to believe that the situation in Iraq was not worth going to war over; most Americans also reject the idea that Iraq, contrary to the president's claims, is a central front in the war on terror; they largely believe that the costs even of a victory there will outweigh any benefits; and by 2007, they disapproved of President George W. Bush's handling of the war in record numbers, 70 percent to 24 percent.[4] Overseas, the war was always less popular, even among many of America's friends. Bush's closest ally, Tony Blair, has seen his own popularity nosedive much like Bush's and left office in 2007. In an especially embarrassing blow, one of his own ministers—thinking she was speaking off the record— referred in 2006 to Blair's support of the 2003 war as an exercise in "moral imperialism."[5]

The intent here, however, is not to debate whether the invasion of Iraq was wise or justified. The war is still ongoing, and the wounds are still too fresh, for an objective assessment. Worse, the issue has for the time being become impossibly partisan and polarized, creating a climate of debate that inevitably centers on charges and countercharges about the war in what American political scientist Robert Lieber has called a "veritable *reductio ad Iraqum*."[6] Taking a longer view, it is difficult to assess the prudence of going to war in Iraq because wars tend to have long-term unintended consequences, both good and ill, that are not apparent in the heat of battle.[7] Whether the war in Iraq will lead to eventual disaster or victory, however defined, is simply unknowable at this point. Or, as Donald Rumsfeld might put it, using his somewhat contorted taxonomy, the outcome in Iraq is a "known unknown," whose eventual issue is at the mercy of too many "unknown unknowns."

The more immediate question is whether the current mess in Iraq, and public opposition to it, mean that the era of preventive war is over even before it began. Is the situation in Iraq such a fiasco that the United States and other countries around the world have now learned painful lessons about the risks of prevention? Or will Iraq recede into the international collective memory as an ill-advised war that nonetheless says little about how best to handle the threats of a new era? While *The Nation*'s Jonathan Schell saw Iraq in 2004 as showing "the folly of imperial rule in the twenty-first century," conservative columnist David Brooks three years later dismissed any notion of an imminent "Iraq Syndrome" in the United States: "Forget about it. Americans are having a debate about how to proceed in Iraq, but we are not having a strategic debate about retracting American power and influence."[8] Either way, the situation in Iraq has created such general controversy that the European Union's Robert Cooper has suggested that the whole debate over prevention itself might need something of a "cooling off period."[9] Unfortunately, the pace of international events, as ever, is unlikely to allow for that kind of respite, and hard questions will be forced upon nations and their leaders whether they are ready for them or not.

It is impossible to say with any degree of confidence how the public in the United States or elsewhere will respond to the next major international security crisis. Much will depend on exactly what kind of threat is being prevented, against whom it is directed, how much reliable intelligence there is regarding it, what the constellation of political forces in the most militarily capable states might be at the given moment, and so on. But when discussing the problem of preventive war, there is no denying that Iraq is the proverbial elephant in the middle of the room, and so it is worth pausing, even if only briefly, to speculate about what effect the largest preventive war in a century will have on thinking about the subject in the future.

"Neo-Culpa"

In late 2003, George W. Bush gave a private interview to Bob Woodward of the *Washington Post*. Woodward pressed Bush on why, after several months of occupation, coalition forces had failed to turn up any actual

weapons of mass destruction. Showing the influence of preventive thinking, Bush argued that even the possibility that there were WMD hidden
in Iraq meant that action had to be taken against Saddam Hussein,
"given his nature."[10] In his account, Woodward notes that it took Bush
over five minutes just to acknowledge that no WMD had been found,
but the president remained convinced of the threat: "The person who
wants the president to stand up and declare that publicly is also the person who wants to say, Shouldn't have done it." Tellingly, Bush added:
"I'm probably sounding incredibly defensive all of a sudden."[11] But
throughout the 2004 election and into his second term, the president
was steadfast in arguing that Operation Iraqi Freedom was necessary.

But just a few years after the fall of Baghdad, others—even of the president's own party and ideological affiliation—were no longer as sure.
The most striking change of heart about the use of force has come from
some prominent American public intellectuals who for many years
urged an attack on Iraq. Collectively, they are dubbed "neoconserva-
tives," but that is to some extent a misnomer; originally, the so-called
"neocons" were liberal Democrats who had crossed over to conserva-
tism, breaking with the American left largely over the issue of relations
with the Soviet Union and support for the state of Israel. (As one of the
original neocons, Irving Kristol, often quipped, he and others like him
thought of themselves as "liberals who had been mugged by reality.")
The label has since become more or less content-free as used in American public debate, most often appearing as shorthand by critics of the
war to refer to those in favor of it. Insofar as it denotes a school of
thought about foreign policy, Ambassador Kenneth Adelman, a self-
identified neoconservative, describes it as "the idea of a tough foreign
policy on behalf of morality, the idea of using our power for moral good
in the world."[12]

It most strongly remains attached to a group of conservative intellectuals both in and out of government since the late 1980s who for some
time had pressed successive American administrations to depose Saddam Hussein. With Iraq now in the midst of civil war, some of those
thinkers have come to reconsider their positions. British writer David
Rose (himself an initial supporter of the invasion) conducted a startling
series of interviews with many of them for *Vanity Fair*, and dubbed their
doubts a "neo-culpa."[13]

The views of this group, which include Adelman, former G. W. Bush
speechwriter David Frum, former Reagan administration Pentagon offi-

cials Richard Perle and Frank Gaffney, and other prominent conserva-tives, are important, as they provided much of the intellectual framework for the invasion of Iraq. (They were not, however, the actual planners for Operation Iraqi Freedom. Perle rightly complained to Rose, "I'm getting damn tired of being described as an architect of the war.")[14] Many of them are still relatively young, and can be expected to be part of any debate in the future over the use of force.

The main question is whether the travails of OIF have soured them on the war in Iraq specifically or on the discretionary use of violence in general. As Joshua Muravchik, a conservative scholar at the American Enterprise Institute, put it in an interview with the *Washington Post* in late 2006, "There's a question to be sorted out: whether the war was a sound idea but very badly executed."[15] While the war's former proponents are willing to engage in self-criticism for poor assessments of the situation in Iraq, almost all in the end charge the Bush administration with dire incompetence in executing what might have been a good idea.

Adelman, who famously once said that defeating the Iraqi military would be "a cakewalk," later wondered if war, however justified, was the right instrument to use against Saddam. If asked again what his advice would have been, he answered:

The policy itself can be absolutely right, and noble, beneficial, but if you can't execute it, it's useless, just useless. I guess that's what I would have said: Bush's arguments are absolutely right, but you know what? You just have to put them in the drawer marked CAN'T DO. And that's very different from LET'S GO. (emphasis original)

But Adelman nonetheless blames the Bush administration and what he calls one of "the most incompetent [national security] teams in the post-war era" for its handling of the war once the decision was made to move forward. [16] Although he initially kept his concerns out of the public arena, he was supposedly forced to resign from the Pentagon's Defense Policy Board after a reportedly "furious" confrontation with Donald Rumsfeld, but other accounts claim that he survived Rumsfeld's even-tual 2006 ouster as defense secretary and remained on the Board.[17]

Perle, for his part, admits that he "underestimated the depravity" and "brutality" that the war brought to Iraq, but also lays the blame on Bush and his advisors for their "disastrous" and confused decision-making processes, marked by internal opposition and even "disloyalty."[18] Perle's volte-face on prevention, at least as applied to Iraq, is striking. Although he still maintains that he was correct in his initial fears that Iraq could at some point produce WMD and give them to terrorists, he now believes that the threat could have been "managed" by "means other than a direct military intervention."[19]

But does this mean that this influential group of American foreign policy intellectuals now rejects the preventive premises of the war itself? Perhaps, although some of them seem to worry more about whether the war in Iraq is going to make other Americans more squeamish about using force in situations where it might be necessary. Adelman is particularly concerned that the moral direction at the heart of the broader neoconservative philosophy, "of using American strength for good in the world," is going to suffer. "I don't think [it's] disproven by Iraq. But it's certainly discredited."[20] Muravchik is more direct and more pessimistic: "That part of our plan is down the drain."[21] They are not alone in these concerns. Michael Glennon has wondered if the "greater danger after the second Persian Gulf War is not that the United States will use force when it should not, but that, chastened by the war's horror, the public's opposition, and the economy's gyrations, it will not use force when it should."[22] James Traub also fears that skepticism engendered by the failures of OIF could be dangerous: "The next time someone cries wolf, there really may be a wolf."[23]

Others, like James Woolsey, Bill Clinton's CIA director and a supporter of the invasion of Iraq, still thought, as of late 2006, that something like victory is possible in Iraq.[24] But Eliot Cohen of Johns Hopkins University (appointed a counselor to Secretary of State Condoleezza Rice in 2007), another influential conservative voice in favor of the war, described his mood to David Rose as "pretty grim. I think we're heading for a very dark world, because the long-term consequences of this are very large, not just for Iraq, not just for the region, but globally—for our reputation, for what the Iranians do, all kinds of stuff."[25] The Iranians loom large in such calculations, and for good reason: anything that looks like a U.S. defeat in Iraq could well bring about a greater chance of confrontation with an emboldened Iran. This would lead to a military confrontation with Tehran just as the Americans, supposedly, would be least likely to want to pursue one. Frank Gaffney is particularly pessimistic in this regard: "I would say that the likelihood of military action against Iran is 100 percent. I just don't know when or under what circumstances. My guess is that it will be in circumstances of their choosing and not ours."[26]

Iraq, Iran, and "Iraq-Like Actions"

There is plenty of trouble in the world, and the Western security agenda has more than enough items to occupy the United States and its allies, especially in the wake of Iraq. But where the problem of preventive war is concerned, the ongoing struggle with the Iranians over their nuclear program is the most likely test case in the near future of whether the war in Iraq has really pushed prevention back into the cage of disrepute in which it was for so long held. As of early 2007, there is no indication that diplomatic efforts are succeeding in stopping or even slowing the Iranian pursuit of nuclear weapons. To the contrary, Iran's leaders remain defiant; although Iranian president Mahmood Ahmadinejad was rebuked in local elections in Iran in December 2006, the defeat of his candidates probably expressed more displeasure with his extremist rhetoric and provocations of the West than with Iran's attempt to become a nuclear-armed state, which in any case predated Ahmadinejad's presidency.[27] At some point—estimates differ by five to ten years—the great powers, particularly the United States and the European Union, may well face a moment of truth as Iran prepares to cross the threshold to become, after North Korea, the second new nuclear power of the twenty-first century.[28] (This assumes, of course, that the Israelis don't first obviate the whole question by taking matters into their own hands.)

Some see a new reticence in Washington about prevention that can be traced directly to the troubles in Iraq.[29] Francis Fukuyama, who publicly broke with the neoconservative movement shortly after the invasion of Iraq, argued in 2005 that the Bush administration had already learned its lesson and that the Bush Doctrine was a dead letter:

The best way to assess the durability of the Bush doctrine is to ask how likely it is to be applied again in the future—that is, how ready is the US to again intervene unilaterally to topple a rogue state proliferator and engage in another nation-building exercise? The answer comes from the Bush administration itself, which has already backed away from military confrontations with both North Korea and Iran in favor of multilateral approaches, despite much clearer evidence of nuclear programs in those countries. This suggests the doctrine has not survived into Mr. Bush's second term, much less become a permanent component of US strategy against global terrorism.[30]

Fukuyama is certainly correct that the Bush administration, bogged down in Iraq, is hardly likely to propose new ground invasions of rogue states, not least because the Americans would either have to quit Iraq or go out and rent an army to do another major military operation like OIF. But a closer reading shows that Fukuyama has, in a sense, stacked the deck: he claims only that the United States is unlikely to engage in unilateral regime change, going it alone to take down a foreign government and then rebuilding the target nation from scratch. Fukuyama might well have argued that no administration, of either party, is going to suggest any such thing in the near future.

But does that realization tell us very much about whether notions of prevention have been scrapped in Washington or anywhere else? If the war in Iraq is a unique case, at least as a template for future military action, it could mean that threats to the international system will not only overwhelm the heated politics of the moment, but also overpower partisan differences in the United States and other nations on the question of prevention.

This is an important point, because a significant problem in trying to extrapolate from OIF is that comparisons between the situation Iraq on the one hand, and challenges in North Korea or Iran on the other, are strategically meaningless. War with North Korea, for example, would eventually result in a U.S.-South Korean victory, something even the densest North Korean military planner probably understands. But that is not the point: any war in Korea would first mean the utter destruction of the South Korean capital. The North Koreans have the capacity both with missiles and men to maintain an offensive that will reach the southern capital and lay waste to it. Nicholas Eberstadt warns that "Pyongyang can always remind the Blue House (South Korea's presidential residence) that the enormous metropolis of Seoul is a hostage to fate, to be destroyed in a moment on Kim Jong Il's say-so."[31] A second Korean war might yet still come—and one can only hope that the north's generals understand what such a war would mean, even if the Dear Leader does not—but it is flawed reasoning to ask why the U.S. and its allies would be willing to topple Saddam Hussein but not Kim Jong Il. The costs of such a war would be horrendous, with casualties measured in the millions.

This is not to say that a violent conflict with Pyongyang is impossible, but rather to point out that the war in Iraq has little to offer as a guide to thinking through calculations about how to remove North Korea's nuclear potential. And as it turns out, Operation Iraqi Freedom has not blunted calls, at least from some quarters, for military action against the North, despite tremendous risks, if all else fails. The possibility of military action is emphasized particularly by Clinton administration officials who endured the 1994 crisis with the North Koreans.

For example, Graham Allison, who served as assistant secretary of defense in 1993 and 1994, wrote in 2004: "Horrific as the consequences of a preemptive attack would be"—although clearly, such an attack would be preventive, rather than preemptive—"the prospect of a nuclear North Korea willing to sell its weapons to al Qaeda and other terrorists would be worse."[32] Two years later, Clinton's secretary of defense, William Perry, and one of his former deputies, Ashton Carter, ran out of patience with Pyongyang as North Korea prepared to test the three-stage, intercontinental-range Taepodong missile capable of reaching the United States. (This was the second attempt to launch a missile capable of reaching North America, and the second time it fell short; the Taepodong-2 would perhaps be better named the "Go-wrong 2" for now.) Using the purest language of prevention, Perry and Carter argued that "diplomacy has failed, and we cannot sit by and let this deadly threat mature," and that the missile should be attacked and destroyed on its launch pad if North Korea continued test preparations.[33]

Iran, too, is a much different kind of problem from Iraq. The United States and the regime in Tehran are avowed enemies, and for good reason. Iran not only is trying to acquire nuclear arms, but is a proven state sponsor of terror. Indeed, when it comes to international mischief, Iran during the past two decades has arguably been a far worse problem than Iraq. But Iran is not the absolute and personalized dictatorship that Iraq was under Saddam, nor are its leaders unanimous in their policies. And Iran, while a repressive theocracy, is not the charnel-house Iraq became under the Baathists. There are elements of Iranian society that are pro-Western and who disapprove of the manic rhetoric of their own president, and there is reason to believe that change is possible in Iran. An invasion, even if one could be launched against a country of some 70 million people, would accomplish nothing and short-circuit any possibility of peaceful regime change, which was fundamentally impossible in totalitarian Iraq.

More to the point, accepting that it would be foolish to invade Iran or North Korea is not the same as rejecting any kind of military action at all against their nuclear programs. The European Union has tried, however unsteadily, to build pressure on the Iranians to halt their nuclear program, uniting opposition to the Iranians while still leaving open military options.[34] To argue the matter in terms of the costs of invasion, particularly in the Iranian case, is not only pointless but even disingenuous. If military action were to be taken against Iran's nuclear program, it would largely happen in the air, and it would end with satellite imagery of destroyed bunkers and laboratories rather than with American troops marching into Tehran and tearing down posters of the Ayatollah Khomeini or pulling President Ahmadinejad from some Saddam-like spider hole.

Finally, the rhetoric from George Bush's would-be successors regarding Iran does not suggest that the Iraq war has dampened enthusiasm for preventive action, at least in American political debate. While Republican candidate John McCain allowed that his support for the Iraq war may have destroyed his presidential chances, if not his entire political career, his competitors see no harm in talking tough about Iran.[35] Presidential candidates in the United States, including those who have been relentlessly critical of the Bush administration's handling of Iraq such as former senator and 2004 vice-presidential nominee John Edwards, insist that that military force must remain an open option in dealing with Iran. Edwards was in fact so emphatic about stopping the Iranian nuclear program that he prompted criticism across the spectrum: journalist Ari Berman, in his blog at *The Nation*, complained that "George W. Bush is upping the ante towards a war with Iran. And a number of prominent Democrats seem to be telling the President to go all in," while the editors of *al-Jazeera* predictably depicted Edwards as an Israeli puppet and exhorted readers to "pray and make sure that Edwards may never be elected."[36] Edwards has been joined in this kind of rhetoric by other candidates like Democratic New York senator Hillary Clinton and Republican Massachusetts governor Mitt Romney, who traded accusations about who, in effect, would be quicker to get tough on Iran.[37]

This may be an attempt among presidential hopefuls to burnish their national security credentials, as the more savvy ones often do, but it may also be a natural reaction to public fears about the changed security environment in the early twenty-first century. John Gaddis argued in 2005 that "neither Bush nor his successors, whatever their party," can ignore the lessons of 9/11.[38] Robert Lieber likewise contends that

over the long term any American administration, whether Democratic or Republican, will need to adopt a national security strategy that largely incorporates key elements of . . . the Bush doctrine. The chief difference will be that the next president, whether a Democrat or Republican, will call that doctrine by another name.[39]

In any case, to say that Western nations are cautious about invading other countries is not to say very much about whether their governments are willing to use other kinds of force in situations they perceive as highly threatening. But the larger question still remains. Will the citizens of the Western democracies, after Iraq, be willing to risk their sons and daughters in yet more military interventions of any kind against rogue states?

First and foremost, when faced with claims that their nation is in danger, will voters even believe it? The failure of intelligence before OIF was massive and widespread, as a later analysis noted:

the United States and Iraq were not the only ones that erred. How does one account for the fact that so many foreign intelligence services were also apparently wrong about Iraq's pre-war WMD capabilities and programs? No Western or Middle Eastern intelligence service is known to have dissented from Washington's assessment of Iraq's WMD capabilities and potential before the war.[40]

Of course, the world's intelligence officers cannot shoulder all the blame, since one of the more vexing problems with trying to figure out what was going in Iraq was that Saddam Hussein himself, for some reason, was acting as if he had WMD that he presumably knew did not exist. But the fact that the single strongest claim for war against Saddam turned out to be unfounded means, as French diplomat Errera put it, that both the United States and the West in general have, for the time being, "lost the benefit of the doubt" should they try to convince their own citizens or other nations, particularly in the less developed world, to support preventive actions.[41] As U.S. weapons inspector David Kay admitted in 2004, "If you cannot rely on good, accurate intelligence that is credible to the American people and to others abroad, you certainly can't have a policy of preemption."[42] Why, after being once bitten in Iraq, wouldn't most people be twice shy about prevention elsewhere?

Again, this is to some extent an unfair question, since we cannot know what kind of threat, what kind of evidence, or what kind of arguments (or by whom) will be presented to voters. A hysterical North Korean denunciation of Japan, followed by photographs of the unmistakable vapor clouds that indicate the preparation of a liquid-fueled missile, is not the same thing as the coy assertions of Iranian officials that their nuclear program is only for the peaceful production of electricity. Uncovering a verified terrorist training camp in Africa would not merit the same response as the discovery of a terrorist money laundering operation in some tiny nation in the Caribbean.

But there is some indication of how people, at least in the United States and Europe, regard further interventions as a general matter. The evidence suggests that the problem created by the war in Iraq is not so much an aversion to military action, but rather the strong disapproval of *unilateral* military action, especially by the United States.

This is an especially interesting finding, considering that Operation Iraqi Freedom was not strictly a unilateral action. While only four nations (the U.S., UK, Poland, and Australia) contributed combat forces to the actual invasion—with the American contingent dwarfing the other three—there was significant support for the invasion, at least on paper, from several governments that later provided troops to postwar operations. Some of this, as writer William Shawcross later pointed out, was in part out of conviction, but also driven by a fear that without allies, the Americans would feel the need to go it alone, which in turn raised concerns about the unrestrained use of U.S. power:

What [Tony] Blair really feared above all else was America being driven into isolationism. There were many other governments—Italy, Romania, Bulgaria, Poland, Australia, Spain, are only a few—which feared the same and believed also that the United States was right to take military action at this time against Saddam. . . . In Europe, Blair could point out that despite the posturing of France, Germany, Belgium, and Luxembourg, most governments supported Washington. . . . By September 2003, more than thirty countries (besides the U.S. and UK) had 16,000 troops on the ground in Iraq.[43]

But while allied *governments* supported the war, their peoples either opposed it or were deeply ambivalent about it, particularly because it took place without UN sanction. The invasion, despite the statements of international support that surrounded it, looked to most people like a strictly American production. Unlike Kosovo, it would not even enjoy the blessing of NATO. This perception of American unilateralism is perhaps the most important legacy of the war in Iraq, at least in terms of international support for future preventive actions.

There is at least some evidence, however, that this disaffection with preventive action is not permanent, especially if the problem of unilateralism is more or less solved somehow. Polls indicate, for example, that restoring the role of international organizations seems to restore the support of previous opponents of preventive actions. In 2004, a year after the invasion of Iraq (and with trouble clearly in sight there), Americans and Europeans were asked if they would support "military action in a future Iraq-like situation with international approval by the UN." What exactly an "Iraq-like" situation might look like was left undefined, but it is probably a safe assumption that most people hearing that expression would think of large-scale military action, and perhaps even regime change, against a rogue state. The important part of the question was the stipulation of United Nations approval, and when asked in that way, 82 percent of Europeans indicated their willingness to support another such action, far higher than the 58 percent who agreed in the United States.[44] Even more revealing, however, is that the poll respondents did not enshrine the United Nations as the sole or ultimate source of authority for the use of force: 80 percent of Europeans would also approve of such an action if were supported by their main European allies, while 72 percent would require only the approval of NATO. The Americans agreed, but by smaller majorities, with the approval of major U.S. allies more important to Americans than either NATO or the UN.

In other words, the Americans in the survey tended to show their attraction to unilateral solutions, while the Europeans, belying the stereotype of passivity, showed a willingness to fight, even after Iraq, but not without the sanction of the UN, NATO, or their closest allies, in that order. As French scholar Pascal Boniface argued in 2003, "regime change can at times in fact be an acceptable practice, but only with multilateral approval," and he chided Americans for not understanding that "impatience and inconvenience are not sufficient reasons to weaken international order through unilateral action."[45] Nor were Europeans averse to helping in Iraq even in the postwar chaos if asked by the United Nations: the Marshall study noted that Europeans were "surprisingly supportive" of keeping their troops in Iraq under a UN mandate, "despite a very difficult spring [2004] in Iraq."[46]

In 2006, the Marshall Fund dropped the question about "Iraq-like" actions, and got right to the problem of what to do about Iran's attempts to gain nuclear weapons. Again, the answers pointed to a greater acceptability of a preventive solution—*if all else fails*—than might have been expected in the wake of the Iraq imbroglio. By majorities of more than 80 percent, virtually all of Europe (with the usual exception of Turkey) agreed that efforts should continue to thwart the Iranian acquisition of nuclear arms, with some Europeans feeling even more strongly on the subject than the Americans. When asked what options should be taken if all diplomatic and other nonviolent options are exhausted, majorities only in the United States, France, and Portugal supported military action, with the French by a small margin actually the most supportive. But a focus only on absolute majorities obscures a much more interesting result in the Marshall data: the use of force against Iran as a last resort enjoys the support of strong *pluralities* (45 percent or more) in Britain, Italy, the Netherlands, and Spain; by contrast, those willing to live with an Iranian bomb are in marked minorities in every country surveyed.[47]

Put another way, if a vote were held in Western Europe—the area that would face the most immediate threat from future Iranian missiles—over whether to destroy the Iranian nuclear program by force as a last resort, more Europeans overall would be in favor rather than against, however conflicted or reluctant they might be about such a course of action. The war in Iraq may have made the Europeans (to say nothing of the Americans) more likely to resist unilateral American invasions of other nations, but it seems to have had little effect on the willingness of significant numbers of people in the United States and the European Union to countenance some sort of military action, preferably under the UN banner, perhaps with NATO's authorization, or even with just the support of their closest friends, against a rogue nuclear program once all other avenues have been exhausted.

No More Iraqs . . . But More Yemens?

Actually, in assessing the impact of the war in Iraq on the prevention debate, a major invasion like Operation Iraqi Freedom is something of a red herring in the whole matter. To be sure, the very term "preventive war" conjures up images of a huge military force invading and occupying another country. But to ask if the major powers will support more operations like Iraq is to ask the wrong question. Regime change would doubtless be the very rarest kind of military action in the age of prevention. Totalitarian dictatorships like Baathist Iraq, because they are unable to reform peacefully, are likelier candidates for regime change when they become a threat beyond their borders or begin the massive extermination of innocents, but examples of such states are few and far between. Rather, more plausible dilemmas will involve smaller-scale operations resembling the 1981 Israeli raid on the Iraqi nuclear reactor, the various American cruise missile strikes in Iraq and elsewhere in the 1990s, or the use of covert operations, commandos, or other specialized forces.

In 2002, for example, the United States killed a group of terrorists in Yemen without involving any actual soldiers. American intelligence officials spotted a car in a remote area carrying six men, including al-Qaeda's top operative in Yemen (believed to be the organizer of the attack on the USS *Cole*), along with five associates, all suspected al-Qaeda members. An unmanned drone operated by the Central Intelligence Agency fired a single missile at the car, killing all six. Although the government of Yemen gave its permission for the operation, it was a formality: the Americans, it was later revealed, had told the Yemenis that the operation was going to take place one way or another.[48] Predictably, the United States described the strike as a tactical operation in an ongoing war with a terrorist organization; just as predictably, critics charged that it constituted the summary execution of six suspects without trial or jury. (An "act of war," and "cold-blooded murder," the *London Guardian* thundered.)[49]

The outcry about the strike, however, was limited, and the international community, so far as it took notice, generally accepted the legitimacy of the attack. One British scholar, perhaps yielding to the obvious, later suggested that the lack of any serious international opposition to the Yemen incident might point to the emergence of new norms that are more accepting of both "targeted killings" in particular and smaller-scale military operations in general.[50] But whether the attack in Yemen is viewed as a quick success in an ongoing war, or a barbaric assassination by a swaggering superpower, such incidents are likely to be more frequent. The major chaos in Iraq is not likely to figure in discussions of actions that are tiny by comparison.

But small is not necessarily always beautiful, and even small operations will have large implications. In Stephen Krasner's meditation on what might happen should there be incidents of nuclear terrorism in the West, he suggests that preventive strikes such as the Yemen operation would become "widely accepted," and that the "country launching the strike would not be expected to request permission from the target country."[51] Clearly, we are closer to Krasner's imagined world than we realize. Had the Yemen strike taken place even over the objections of the Yemeni government, as it would have, this itself would have constituted an armed attack on the territory of a foreign nation, otherwise known as "war."

The sheer size of OIF is also misleading in thinking about future military actions. Even large operations, whether as preventive actions or humanitarian interventions—or possibly both—will not require military investments the size of that needed to topple Saddam Hussein in 2003. The commanding general of the UN peacekeepers in Rwanda, for example, at the height of the genocide only asked for 5,000 troops, a small force, but one he believed could have stopped the massacres.[52] (Others have contested this number as too small, but even twice as many soldiers still represents a relatively small operation.)[53] Likewise, dousing the civil war in Somalia in the early 1990s—admittedly a temporary victory, but one that unraveled for political rather than military reasons—took fewer than 40,000 soldiers, roughly less than a quarter of the number of troops initially engaged in the occupation of Iraq. Operations that aim to secure or destroy particular targets, rather than to change a regime or enforce a peace, would logically entail even fewer assets, and in some cases might not require the presence of human military personnel at all. There was little objection in the past, for example, to things like American cruise missile strikes, and there is no reason to believe there will be any greater objections after Iraq.

None of this is to say that any of these actions will be accomplished without complications, unintended consequences, or the deaths of innocent civilians. Friction and confusion are immutable characteristics of military conflict. But they are well within the military capabilities of the great powers, and they can be executed without necessarily triggering debates that will raise the specter of Operation Iraqi Freedom. As Martha Finnemore points out, few people even see such small-scale operations as "wars":

intervention policies lie at the boundary of peace and war in international politics. Deploying military force against another state is obviously not peaceable activity, yet states take great pains to distinguish these actions from war . . . .That a formal declaration of war was not made seems a trivial distinction, yet we take the distinction very seriously. No one talks about recent U.S. wars with Somalia or Grenada. Americans would bristle (or laugh) at the notion that these actions were war, yet most would be hard pressed to explain why, exactly, they were something else.[54]

The invasion of Iraq may have made the United States more reticent about another major commitment of troops to the invasion and occupation of a rogue state, but there is little evidence that events in Iraq will dissuade any of the great powers from taking smaller and more manageable actions.

These more limited operations will be dressed, as they are now, in the stodgy gray tones of bureaucratic language: they will be called "targeted killings," "precision strikes," "short-duration incursions," or any number of awkward euphemisms. But no matter what they are called, many of them will unmistakably fall into a broader and more encompassing category: "acts of war." Whether the international community will allow them to take place at the whim of the strongest powers, or instead find a way somehow to regulate them in the name of international security, will be the central question in the new age of prevention.

Chapter 6
Governing the New Age of Prevention

Renunciation of war as a method of settling disputes between the "civilized" powers remains. But an attempt is now underway to pacify the disordered parts of the world, springing from a mixture of fear, self-interest and moralism. Yesterday's peaceniks are transformed into today's warriors.

—Lord Robert Skidelsky, 2004

Delusions of an invincible superpower have perished in the sands of Mesopotamia. But what will emerge after the fantasy of the unipolar moment perishes? Like it or not—and many Americans will dislike it intensely—part of the solution will be the United Nations.

—British journalist Martin Wolf, 2007

Back to the Future

The anxieties of the early twenty-first century are evident. The French president threatens nuclear retaliation against state sponsors of terror. His Russian counterpart makes thunderous vows to strike first at any threats to Russia anywhere on the planet. The Ethiopians, with Western assent, invade a neighbor and quash a possible enemy regime. The Japanese debate whether to eradicate North Korea's growing nuclear threat by force. The Australians call for amending the United Nations charter to allow strikes on terrorists. The British prime minister chides those who wish "to err on the side of caution" and "weigh the risks to an infinite balance." And the U.S. government publishes a National Security Strategy that argues that "the United States can no longer solely rely on a reactive posture" nor "let our enemies strike first."

The age of prevention is upon us.

We don't have to like that fact, but we do have to deal with it. The status quo, the set of institutional arrangements and informal understandings that have more or less constrained the use of force since World War II, will in short order be impossible to maintain. The previous pillars of that order, ranging from the traditions—even if often unenforceable—of international law to the more concrete law of deterrence, no longer promise the protection they once did. As journalist David Ignatius put it after the North Korean detonation of a nuclear device in October 2006, the Korean bomb test "is a seismic event for the world community. It tells us that the structure created to maintain global security is failing."[1] And so it is. The question remains now of what will replace it.

The two likeliest possibilities for the future are each disturbing in its own way, and each risks the anarchy of centuries past. A third road is more promising, even if less probable.

The first outcome is the world as it is (or has been for about a decade or so now), in which we continue to pretend that the status quo is viable, while states attack threats to themselves, and notionally, to the international order, through the use of ad hoc and unilateral violence. This would be the least stable alternative, in part because threats to the status quo would likely end up being dealt with only erratically by the major powers, who would organize the equivalent of international posses and take selective action depending on the interests and beliefs of the coalition of the moment. More worrisome, threats that are *not* dealt with could end up being more dangerous than those that are. The strongest powers might forgo military action if they do not see a particular threat to their own people—or if they have ceased to care very much about the welfare of others in an anarchic international situation that is a "system" in name only. This is already a problem, as Robert Skidelsky notes.

Rogue states are latent threats to the security of others, producing a demand for preventive war. Failed states produce humanitarian disasters. The result is either that these problems are dealt with outside the UN framework, as in the Iraq war in 2003, or they are not dealt with at all, as in Rwanda in 1994.[2]

A suspect chemical plant could be destroyed in a matter of days, but a massive famine, a widening civil war, or an engineered genocide that produces chaos and dislocation—perhaps enough to shelter terrorist organizations and obscure their activities amidst all the bloodshed— might not be acted upon at all.

Another possibility is that the great powers will increasingly grant to each other the exceptional right to use violence as they will, reinventing a kind of nineteenth-century congress of the great powers. This would be a final acknowledgment of the reality that the whole arrangement of the international system after World War II was always about stability rather than justice. To be sure, there is much to be said for stability, since without it there is no hope of justice in any case. Still, this would be a world in which the strong, by mutual assent, will indeed do what they can and the weak will suffer what they must, with the most powerful nations consenting among themselves to breaches of the peace out of an unspoken fear that each of them might be the one needing to use force the next time around. Such an arrangement would probably satisfy no one completely, but would, for most of the time, keep the peace—or at least limit the damage of war. The goal in such a world will be to avert anarchy and to keep the carnage to a minimum.

But there are two major risks to such an outcome. One is that smaller nations will be faced with a system based on coercion rather than comity, and might well resent it. This would not be a community of nations, so much as an arrangement of convenience among the strong. The smaller states, the democracies among them, would be forced to accept the situation—the dictatorships will reject it under any circumstances—and thus sign on to an international order that contradicts their own values. A related problem is that the cure might be as bad as the disease. While this kind of great power compact would represent a short-term defeat for enemies of the status quo, the political damage to ideas of the rule of law and the just use of force might be so great that in the long run rogues and terrorists might welcome seeing the great liberal democracies betray their own ideals in the name of security.

Either way, the international order forged after World War II—such that it was—would be gone. At this point in history, it might even be unwise to try to save it. A vain attempt to preserve the current order would be a dangerous and cynical course of action. The world of the early twenty-first century is already characterized by a level of hypocrisy that is stunning even by the wince-inducing standards of international politics: previous thinking regarding war and peace has obviously given way to new norms, but rather than face this reality, the old rules are still given a passing nod by the great powers even as they revise their defense doctrines and restructure their armed forces for preventive action. Trying to rescue what is left of an order built from the wreckage of the war against the Axis over a half century ago is a recipe neither for the iron hand of a great power concert nor for cooperative international security. It is the path to anarchy.

If things are left adrift as they are now, the preventive use of force—or really, of any kind of force—will be ungoverned and ungovernable. Powerful nations will resort to ad hoc coalitional actions to keep international order, stop proliferators, change odious regimes, and extinguish genocidal conflicts, running roughshod over the United Nations while claiming, disingenuously or not, to act in the name of international law, the international community, and the integrity of the United Nations. The targets of such violence, for their part, will try to throw fig leaves over their dangerous schemes, pushing nuclear bomb factories or germ laboratories behind innocent-looking industrial facades, or insisting that the deaths of thousands, maybe even millions, might just be the result of a harmless accident and is no one's business anyway.

There is a third alternative: the world as it might be, with significant reform of international institutions and particularly of the United Nations. In this outcome, the most capable members of the system, both great and small, would agree on the broad shape of international security, including enforcing a fundamental respect for human rights. Of course, even in such a world, the strongest nations will bear the burden of action. No matter where we find ourselves in twenty or thirty years, the most important geopolitical reality will still hold true, that when it comes to the defense of international peace and security, the strong will decide what will be done and how. Their interests will often prevail, as they do today. But if their actions are mediated, shaped, and in the end sanctioned, by an institution composed of nations who represent liberal values, then something like a just international order might be kept.

But this will not happen spontaneously. History repeatedly teaches the obvious lesson that strong nations are not always prudent in the exercise of their power, and we should at least try to think through ways in which the immense military might of the greatest powers can be constrained and harnessed for the greatest good. Even those nations that sincerely seek the preservation of peace and the eventual victory of humanistic values can often find themselves on that well-known road paved with good intentions, heading where it always leads.

The United Nations: A "September 10" Organization?

The obvious candidate for governing the new age of prevention is an organization on the East River in Manhattan that, depending on one's view, is either the last, best hope of mankind or the world's most expensive coffee shop full of chattering dilettantes. No institution on the planet is more widely reviled or revered. But for better or worse, the United Nations still exists, and its members, at least in principle, so far still agree to take their disputes to New York rather than to the battlefield. Why can the UN not step in and restore at least some kind order to this international-free-for-all? After all, despite its manifest failures, the UN can claim at least some successes, even after 9/11; it passed a number of resolutions obligating its members to cooperate against terrorism, and did not obstruct the American-led attack against the Taliban in Afghanistan. Why assume that the United Nations and its members cannot rise to the occasion and meet the challenges of the twenty-first century?

The unfortunate answer is that it was never intended to manage such problems, much less solve them. As Skidelsky observed in 2004, "the UN system was not set up to deal with the problems posed by rogue and failed states," a point made nearly a decade earlier by Stanley Hoffmann when he wrote that the UN "is simply not equipped to deal with collapsing states or with rulers who systematically violate human rights."[3] The United Nations was designed not to act but to stall; to force deliberation rather than reach quick consensus. It was never envisioned that the UN would *endorse* military action, but instead, at best, that it might *tolerate* such action under the most narrowly conceived limits. Of course, in the years after World War II, where conflict on a global scale again seemed possible, the dilatory nature of the UN processes made a certain sense. As UN ambassador Henry Cabot Lodge said in a widely quoted 1954 comment: "This organization is created to prevent you from going to hell. It isn't created to take you to heaven." (He also once averred in 1958 that anything the United Nations does that is not aimed at preventing World War III is "at best superfluous.") Judged by that standard, the United Nations clearly contributed to the maintenance of peace, by providing a forum during the Cold War for the superpowers and their various allies and clients to talk, to argue, and sometimes even to listen.

In an echo of Lodge's imagery, foreign policy thinker Walter Russell Mead in 2004 noted that the UN and the Security Council are still caught between by what he calls the "Party of Heaven"—multilateralists like Canada and Germany who traditionally believe in the redeeming power of international institutions—and the "Party of Hell," those great powers like France and Russia who have little interest in institutions per se, and instead prefer the realist game of hardball, especially when it comes to checking the use of American power.[4] Both sides are inconsistent. Because the Party of Heaven demands that military force can only be used with the sanction of international organizations like the Security Council, they in effect throw the question to the Party of Hell, which can be counted on to block effective action in such bodies. The result, Mead writes, is that "in its current form, the Security Council stands for the permanent veto of expediency over principle, of national interest over the common purpose of the human race."[5]

Heaven remains well out of the reach of the United Nations. But can the UN still play any role in keeping the gates of Hell securely locked?

To some extent, this is no longer the main question facing the United Nations. The great powers, including former enemies such as the United States and Russia, have essentially abandoned major interstate warfare—which is all the UN was intended to prevent—as a means of settling disputes, an observation that was once controversial but is now commonplace. As British general Rupert Smith wrote in 2005:

War no longer exists. Confrontation, conflict and combat undoubtedly exist all around the world . . . and states still have armed forces which they use as a symbol of power. None the less, war as cognitively known to most non-combatants, war as battle in a field between men and machinery, war as a massive deciding event in a dispute in international politics: such war no longer exists.[6]

Henry Kissinger has likewise noted that "contrary to historical experience . . . what used to be called the 'great powers' have nothing to gain by military conflict with each other. They are all more or less dependent on the global economic system."[7] Of course, the hymn that "the great powers have outgrown war" is a song the world has heard sung before, usually just in advance of a ghastly explosion of international violence that shatters what in retrospect seems like a lot of silly talk about the durability of peace. But this is not an argument that war has vanished from the international system; rather only that the globe-spanning wars we saw in the twentieth century are no longer likely, even if they remain theoretically possible. The United Nations, in other words, remains designed as the solution to a particular problem that no longer exists.

This not to say that eternal peace has arrived, but rather that it is hard—not impossible, just difficult—to think of a *casus belli* large enough to trigger a war of any significant size between the major powers. There is the nagging problem of China's claims to Taiwan, of course, which could provide the spark for a U.S.-Chinese confrontation should the People's Republic resort to force. But the Chinese are not fools, and they surely know that in destroying Taiwan they would be killing a goose that lays a fair number of golden eggs. Even without a nuclear exchange, the economic damage done to all sides by such a war would be immense. While it is always possible that some renegade communist general will get too enthusiastic about proving China's military might—Beijing's 2006 test of an anti-satellite weapon has all the earmarks of exactly that kind of militaristic puffery—it is difficult to fathom how either side could see itself as better off after a major war in the Pacific.[8]

There is even less potential for war between the other major powers. Although Russian President Vladimir Putin has growled about NATO expansion and the placement of American missile defenses in central Europe, there is nothing at issue, other than irritation, between the Western powers and Russia (which, as a G-8 member, is itself supposedly a "Western power" now). Putin's intemperate outburst in early 2007 about the unilateral and aggressive nature of U.S. foreign policy, comments that might have triggered a crisis two decades earlier, now only prompted American defense secretary Robert Gates to quip, with a smile, that "one Cold War was quite enough."[9] Moscow and Washington, for all their occasional sniping at each other, actually have a great many security problems in common, with terrorism chief among them. Their relations, while sometimes testy, are still recognizable as normal interaction between two competing but peaceful states.[10] Large interstate wars may not be extinct, but they are extremely unlikely in a globalized world. (Surely, we'd probably all be a lot safer if nuclear planners in Moscow, Washington, and Beijing would internalize that reality, but what military organizations plan for, and what political leaders are willing to do, are not often the same thing.)

But if wars among the great powers are improbable, what is left for the United Nations to do? Not much, according to its critics. The perception, especially among Americans, that the organization is dysfunctional, or at the very least outdated, is now widely held, and there is undeniable truth in it. Nor is this is a view limited to traditionally skeptical Americans. Canadian scholar Irving Brecher has written that the United Nations "can be particularly proud of its socio-economic achievements," but "has, in general, performed abysmally on the political, diplomatic, and military fronts."[11] A fellow Canadian, conservative writer Mark Steyn, has referred to the United Nations as a "September

10th organization," incapable of dealing with new threats to world order, and that "to leave Iran or even Darfur in its hands is as ludicrous as Churchill and Roosevelt's fretting over whether they had the League of Nations' approval to launch D-Day."[12] Meanwhile, Russian analyst Andrei Piontkovskii dismisses the UN and the Security Council completely: "The Security Council? Has the Security Council ever defined anything?"[13]

Still, the UN is a popular institution in many countries despite such criticisms, and its defenders might argue that the problem is not the United Nations itself but rather the unwillingness of the major powers to use it. American and British reticence during the Rwandan genocide would be one of the most indicting examples, to say nothing of NATO's evasion of the Security Council during Kosovo. The UN, such reasoning goes, is perfectly capable of taking action against the unholy trinity of humanitarian disasters, proliferation, and terrorism, if only the most privileged and powerful states in the UN could agree among themselves to do it. This requires leadership, and critics of U.S. foreign policy in particular might describe many of the various disasters of the 1990s not as failures of the United Nations, but as failures of American leadership and imagination. In any case, UN supporters would argue, the task, in Gareth Evans's words, is not "to find alternatives to the Security Council as a source of authority, but to make the Security Council work better than it has."[14] As British journalist Martin Wolf has suggested, a "reformed United Nations is at least likely to be more effective than the spasmodic interventions of a solitary and often inattentive super-power."[15]

The central question for the immediate future, then, is whether the new age of prevention will be governed by the United Nations or some other institution, or even a new set of arrangements. So far, we are left with the Charter system mostly from a lack of anywhere better to go. As American legal scholar Anthony Arend has put it, "policymakers could declare the UN Charter framework dead," and admit that "charter law is no longer authoritative and controlling." But to do so, even if it would be "the most intellectually honest approach," would only bring about a situation in which "many states would rejoice at the funeral and take advantage of such a lawless regime," and so the UN Charter system remains, at least theoretically and if only by default, as the arbiter of force.[16]

The Future of the UN

European Union diplomat Robert Cooper summed up the current situation of the United Nations succinctly in 2006: it "is not an organization that runs the world in any meaningful sense." But like many, Cooper finds the United Nations to be an important arena of legitimacy and discussion, and suggests that "if it were abolished, we would have to invent it again."[17]

To be sure, there have been calls, particularly from the American right, simply to abandon the United Nations, even perhaps to abolish it. This kind of absolutism is unrealistic, but there is still a reasonable case to be made that international order is kept not by bureaucrats in New York but by great powers acting in concert when good sense tells them they should. Steyn argues that the world would not miss the UN if it were gone:

> What should replace the UN? Some people talk about a "caucus of the democracies." But I'd like to propose a more radical suggestion: nothing. In the war on terror, America's most important relationships have been not transnational but bilateral: Australia's John Howard didn't dispatch troops to Iraq because the Aussies and the Yanks belong to the same international talking shop; Tony Blair's reliability on war and terror isn't because of the European Union but in spite of it. These relationships are meaningful precisely because they're not the product of formal transnational bureaucracies.[18]

This, however, entails significant risk: vesting faith only in arrangements between the great powers means accepting that the success of each attempt to defuse or settle a threat either to the United States or the larger international community will be a function of whatever governments happen to be in office that day, with each crisis resulting in a search for new friends who might happen to be useful at the moment.

There is also a certain confusion in all this. It is easy to be sympathetic to Steyn's withering description of the United Nations at present as "a shamefully squalid organization whose corruption is almost impossible to exaggerate."[19] But do most of its critics actually wish to see the organization disappear? As writer James Traub asks, even when people speak of moving the UN's functions to some other organization that "works better," this "begs the question: Works better at what?"[20] Is the object to increase the calories consumed by poor children in Africa? To increase literacy among women in Central Asia? To halt forced prostitution in

Eastern Europe? Or is it only to keep the world from blowing itself apart in flinders?

Canadian legal scholar Michael Byers suggests another option, which rejects abandoning the UN but also refuses to take it too seriously in times of grave danger:

> [There is] the intriguing question of whether, in the truly exceptional situation where a serious threat exists, no invitation [to intervene] can be obtained, and the [Security Council] is not prepared to act, states should just simply violate international law without advancing strained and potentially destabilizing legal justifications. States could then allow their action to be assessed subsequently, not in terms of the law, but in terms of its political and moral legitimacy, with a view toward mitigating their responsibility rather than exculpating themselves.[21]

Byers, like Michael Glennon and others, is rightly concerned that putting forward hypocritical legal arguments in times of peril—specious rationales that no one believes but everyone pretends to accept—will do more harm than good to the international order. But there is also the potential for this approach to dissipate into little more than anarchy with ex post facto rationalizations. Such explanations could be especially tricky given that a successful preventive attack might well destroy the kind of exculpatory evidence a state would have presented as requiring action in the first place. This is very similar to Gilles Andréani's "Catholic" interpretation of intervention, in which states admit their sin and later present their reasoning and seek redemption. But it still treats the United Nations as little better than a helpless spectator, left only to applaud politely or bang the desk angrily once the smoke has cleared, with either reaction irrelevant to the way peace is actually being kept.

In any case, the advocates of abandonment or abolition underestimate the degree to which the United Nations itself has become too institutionalized, too deeply embedded in the international community, to simply close up shop. The United States is not going to leave the UN or the Security Council. Whether the Americans will continue to pay for the UN and its many programs, whether the great powers will continue to pretend to care about the General Assembly, or whether they will openly rebel against decisions of the Security Council, are all other matters entirely. But the United Nations, at least for some generations to come, is not going anywhere.

While outright abandonment is not an option, recommendations abound for altering the structure and processes of the institution. The first instinct of bureaucrats when faced with poor institutional performance is to reorganize, as though moving desks around solves the problems created by the people sitting behind them. The United Nations is no different. Several proposals have been floated, particularly regarding the Security Council, that tinker with its size, terms of service, regional makeup, veto powers, and other issues.

These proposals, as scholar Paul Kennedy has noted at length, are unlikely to succeed and instead are invitations to gridlock and grievances:

This is where the fur begins to fly. Would China welcome giving the veto to India and, more particularly, to Japan? One doubts it. Would France and the United Kingdom agree to surrender their single national seat? Unlikely. Could a rotation of European Union states, large and small, bring any consistency of policy to the Security Council's deliberations, if it was Denmark for six months and then Greece, with the larger European powers not occupying a Security Council seat for the next three years or so? Would Russia agree to a Japanese veto? . . . When Germany is mentioned as a front-runner, the Italian government strongly opposes the idea. Pakistan, joined perhaps by other nations in the Muslim world, would be exceptionally uneasy at the scheme to elevate India. Japan's neighbors (quite apart from China) are not enthused by Tokyo's arguments. In Latin America, the assumption that Brazil is the "natural" representative of the region is stoutly denied by Mexico and Argentina; and in Africa, the idea that the Union of South Africa is the obvious choice is contended by Nigeria and Egypt (whose government makes the additional point that no Arab nation possesses a permanent seat). Then there are the objections of the smaller member states, which don't want any additions to the privileged club: Five veto powers are bad enough.[22]

These various proposals are doomed because they are procedural rather than substantive. While some of them might yet be adopted, they will remedy nothing. Trying to solve the problem of Security Council paralysis, for example, by increasing the size of the Council is like trying to solve the problem of violence at hockey games by doubling the size of the teams.[23]

Dithering with organizational rosters might make various nations feel better about their own role in the workings of the UN, but it promises little in terms of getting anything of any importance done.[24] The real dilemma, and the one that few supporters of the United Nations wish to confront, is the immense structural contradiction built into the very constitution of the United Nations: its membership.

Libya, Champion of Human Rights

The main obstacle to the UN emerging as anything like an impartial enforcer of peace and order, to say nothing of justice, is the concept of universal membership, the central tenet of the Charter itself. But as Glennon writes, "the proposition that all [states] are equal is belied by evidence everywhere that they are not—neither in their power, nor in their wealth, nor in their respect for international order or for human rights."[25] The only thing a state must do to gain admittance to the UN is to exist; the internal nature of the regime, unlike, say, in the G-8 or NATO, is of no interest. This leads to counterproductive, even bizarre, outcomes in New York. In 2003, Saddam Hussein's Iraq was slated to chair the UN Conference on Disarmament—a right it earned by being next in alphabetical order—and Moammar Qaddafi's Libya was elected to head the UN Human Rights Commission, later joined there by other noted paladins of liberty like Sudan, Zimbabwe, and China.[26]

A world in which Libya can chair a human rights commission is a world that makes little sense to many people. As the editors of the *New York Times* complained in 2005,

No one can seriously argue that the U.N. is a rationally structured, efficiently managed body. And letting countries like Cuba, Libya and Sudan sit on a human rights commission that judges the records of other countries diminishes the UN's most important authority, its moral authority.[27]

During the Cold War, this sort of thing could be dismissed as just another harmless little *opera bouffe* in the halls of an essentially powerless United Nations. But in an age where states as bad as Libya or worse demand that decisions about the use of force against terrorists and madmen must be made collectively, it isn't quite so funny anymore.

Thus the UN, as it is currently constituted, cannot act as a coherent defender of international order. It is inherently illogical to expect democratic nations and their authoritarian enemies to have a shared vision of international community. Dictators cannot be expected to support the overthrow of dangerous dictators any more than regimes run by religious extremists can be expected to approve violations of national sovereignty aimed at the extermination of terrorist groups who share their ideology. There can be no unanimous constituency for a liberal international order, with its inherent values of peace and human rights, so long as many members of the organization have a vested interested in dictatorship and the brutality that sustains it.

This is particularly true of the General Assembly. The entire atmosphere of the GA emphasizes the reality that the current international order embodied in the United Nations is one in which sordid autocracies can and do thwart the efforts of mature democracies—and worse, do so even while subjecting the ambassadors of those democracies to grating, high-minded speeches about human rights and international justice. Little wonder that when procedural rigging by some of these nations torpedoed a vote in late 2004 to condemn human rights violations in Sudan's Darfur region (as well as abuses in Belarus and Zimbabwe), U.S. Ambassador John Danforth said in frustration: "One wonders about the utility of the General Assembly on days like this."[28] These kinds of shameful moments have produced a kind of international case of cognitive dissonance, in which the admirable goals of institutions like the UN cannot be squared with a feeling that the inmates may be running the asylum.

If the United Nations cannot bring itself to condemn even the horrors of Darfur because such "naming and shaming" will be stopped by reprehensible regimes eager to escape such censure themselves, how can it be expected to exercise actual *force* against such regimes in the future? As Hoffmann has rightly noted: "Too many states among UN members have bloody domestic records, and they can be expected to block any proposal for a forcible collective intervention to change a regime."[29] During the 1994 genocide in Rwanda, for example, one of the rotating seats in the Security Council was held by . . . Rwanda. There was no move to expel it.[30] During the 2003 deliberations about Saddam Hussein's repeated defiance of the Council's demands, another of the rotating seats was held by Syria, itself a Baathist dictatorship like Iraq. If the Security Council must contend with such regimes in its midst, how can it ever be expected to govern the international system where those same regimes are the source of instability and danger?

This situation has led to proposals that neither change the United Nations nor alter the composition of its institutions, but instead simply sidestep the whole mess.

Democracies to the Security Council: Drop Dead

The five permanent members of the United Nations Security Council have always been something of a strange lot. At the moment of its formation in 1945, the Security Council was an exclusive club open only to the major victors over the Axis, and it was the very definition of strange bedfellows. A fading British Empire, an anti-imperialist America, the defeated French, a mortally weakened Nationalist China in the midst of a doomed civil war, and Stalin's nightmarish USSR—itself a totalitarian regime like the Nazi tyranny it had helped to destroy—were all expected somehow to keep the peace while the ashes of World War II were still cooling. Sixty years later, the Security Council can be described as a collection of two former European empires, a massive North American superpower, a fragile Eurasian democracy in recovery from a history of autocracy, and the world's largest country led by a Communist dictatorship. Three are members of the same organization, NATO, that binds together more than a half billion people from some of the richest nations on earth and easily qualifies as the mightiest military force in history. The other two would be relegated to the role of merely regional powers (if even that) were it not for their nuclear arsenals. The security of the world thus rests, at least formally, in the hands of four—or maybe, with Russia still in question, three and a half—democracies, and one autocracy, representing half the six inhabited continents and roughly only a quarter of the world's population.

All five were immediately armed with the power of the veto, and eventually, all gained the power of the atom as well. All are still charged with keeping the peace, a mission that seems as improbable now as it did in the mid-twentieth century. Its record in leading the international community to oppose aggression, from then to now, is poor. As Lieber writes,

The capacity of the United Nations to act, especially in coping with the most urgent and deadly problems, is severely limited, and in this sense, the demand for "global governance" far exceeds the supply. Since its inception in 1945, there have been only two occasions (Korea in 1950 and Kuwait in 1991) when the UN Security Council authorized the use of force, and in both instances the bulk of the forces were provided by the United States.[31]

Supporters of the United Nations rightly point to the brave work done over the years by the "blue helmets," the UN multinational peacekeeping forces. But peace*keeping* is not the same as peace*making*, and the blue helmets have learned the tragic limits to their powers the hard way, as the tortured Pakistanis in Somalia, the overrun Dutch forces in Bosnia, or the slain Belgians in Rwanda can attest. Today, the Security Council really only exists, as it always did, as a "political pact among the Great

Powers, the five permanent members of the Council, to keep the peace among themselves."[32]

Many proposals for reform assume that this strange amalgam of states in the Security Council is flatly unworkable, and thus seek to not to reform the Council but to circumvent it. (No one seems to give much thought to reforming the essentially impotent General Assembly.) By and large, these proposals rely on giving disproportionate power to the world's democracies. Traub explains:

> Over the last few years, scholars, pundits, and critics of the organization have put forward several alternative models: an organization of the major Western states plus India and China; an "Anglosphere" consisting of the United States, the UK, and the Commonwealth; NATO, with a global mandate; a community of liberal democracies.[33]

Note that these are not merely protesting the decisions (or indecision) of the Security Council. They are more drastic solutions that outright avert the authority of the Council and vest the ability to use military force in new structures outside the United Nations by creating shadow bodies that will act when the Council cannot. In all of them, an attempt can be seen to rebuild the international community along some sense of shared values, beliefs, heritage, or culture, or some combination of each. Underlying most of these thought-experiments as well is the belief that democracies, for various reasons, are more peaceful and responsible than other kinds of regimes. Finally, all these alternatives are in a sense revolutionary, in that they reject the idea that all states have the equal and unfettered right to membership in bodies of international governance. This is the ultimate dismissal of the Westphalian concept and its pretense that all states, whether wicked or virtuous, are sovereign equals in the international community. Now, some animals on the farm are to be more equal than others.

Stanley Hoffmann, for example, has proposed a two-step process for ratifying interventions against what he terms clearly "evil" regimes. (Hoffmann is a well-known scholar of European and international affairs, and can hardly be considered an avowed enemy of the United Nations.) In Hoffmann's alternative, the first resort in any proposed intervention would be to the Security Council. But if the Security Council demurs or is paralyzed, Hoffmann proposes a recourse to a new body, the Association of Democratic Nations. This would be composed of NATO and any other

Asian, African, and Latin American liberal democracies, such as India, South Africa, and Chile, as well as Australia and New Zealand. Only liberal democracies would be admitted as members. If such an association approved a collective intervention to change a regime, it would report its reasons and its decisions to the secretary-general of the UN, and could proceed to act.[34]

Thus Hoffmann proposes to reinforce a kind of moral order in which decisions about the use of force would be made not by a legalistic body like the UN, but by an organization whose membership is based on shared democratic and liberal values.

Ivo Daalder and James Lindsay (of the Brookings Institution and the Council on Foreign Relations, respectively) likewise see democracy as the "great dividing line." They argue for an Alliance of Democratic States, made up of

nations with entrenched democratic traditions, such as the United States and Canada; the European Union countries; Japan, South Korea, New Zealand and Australia; India and Israel; Botswana and Costa Rica. Membership would be open to countries where democracy is so rooted that reversion to autocratic rule is unthinkable.[35]

Such an alliance, they argue, would not only be more effective than the Security Council, but could serve as "a powerful instrument for promoting democracy," since states would alter their behavior to seek admission to it, just as they do now with NATO and the European Union. Russian analyst Piontkovskii, in a similar alternative, suggests that the G-8 step in to decide security issues, which would guarantee the participation of the industrial democracies of three continents (while also, of course, ensuring a place at the table for the Russian Federation).[36]

The fracas in the Security Council over Iraq, however, raised questions—and should have—about whether democracies would be all that more effective in policing the planet than anyone else. The debate was one of the ugliest in years, with the United States, in the words of a conservative Republican policymaker, itself acting almost like a "rogue nation," its president unwisely "challenging the Council to make itself relevant" rather than seeking a real debate.[37] Or, as Traub has put it,

In years past, tinhorn dictators, Soviet premiers, and right-wing U.S. senators had occasionally addressed the UN in the bald language of ultimatum, but the leaders of democratic nations had typically been far more respectful. Many of the members sitting there. . .bristled at President Bush's lecture. What's more, although few of them assumed Saddam Hussein's good faith, even fewer of them considered his regime a threat to millions or to world peace, or [to use Bush's words] even a grave and gathering danger.[38]

Actually, all parties to the debate over Iraq did their own particular damage to the prestige and power of the Council. The Bush administration "wanted the legitimacy that comes with UN backing but would not make meaningful concessions in order to gain it," while the French, Germans, and Russians seemed more concerned about constraining American power than about disarming Saddam.[39] Little wonder that UN official Shashi Tharoor later took pains to remind those who have argued for replacing the UN with a coalition of democracies "that during the Iraq debate, the most vigorous resistance to the United States in the council came from other democracies."[40]

Iraq has not been the only case where the democracies have found themselves at odds. In the spring of 2006, the United States tried to put the issue of human rights in Myanmar (the former Burma) on the Security Council's agenda. It was opposed, predictably, by Russia and China, and more surprisingly, by Japan, which had its own reasons for not wanting to get into an imbroglio with an Asian neighbor. Washington was perplexed and angry. A senior advisor to the Bush administration pointed out that on one side of the issue "are China and Russia, which have increasingly repressed civil liberties and democracy over the past two years. On the other side stands every single democracy in the Security Council."[41] Liberal democracies, it seems, have particularistic interests too.

Nor should we forget that democracies, strictly defined, need not always be states that respect the liberal international order, but may be majoritarian tyrannies led by demagogues. These would be no asset to the Security Council; even the normally rowdier General Assembly has shown that it has its own limits with such "democracies." When President Hugo Chávez of Venezuela came to New York in 2006, he personally attacked President Bush, referring to him as the "devil" and complaining that the rostrum still stank of Hell's sulfur.[42] It was a magnificent performance, right down to Chávez making the Sign of the Cross as he stood before the delegates. But it was too over the top, even by the lesser standards of the GA, which has never been reluctant to censure the United States in the strongest terms. "This is everyone's house," an unnamed Latin American diplomat complained, "and a speech like that goes down the same dirty drain as the bitter criticisms of the U.S." Mexico's UN ambassador agreed: "Most members don't want this place to be turned into a mockery. In the General Assembly, there are limits, and he went way beyond them."[43] Chávez's histrionics cost the Venezuelan leader not only credibility but real power: his behavior torpedoed Venezuela's bid for election to the Security Council, which suggests that even the fractious General Assembly can at times be counted upon to act responsibly. (The GA's 2007 refusal to allow Belarus to join the Human Rights Council is another example that might be cause for limited optimism.).

Still, as long as the United Nations cannot act without the approval of regimes that are by their very nature enemies of human rights and a liberal international order, there is no way to salvage any role for it in an age of prevention without significant reform to both its structure and its charter. And salvaged it should be: despite a history of severe, sometimes even buffoonish missteps by its leaders, the UN seeks noble ends and retains a distinct legitimacy in the eyes of many around the world. As Anne-Marie Slaughter has written, "when [the UN] speaks in unison, it projects moral authority that no individual government can match."[44] Soldiers have died in its service, attempting to save the innocent, keep the peace, and maintain something like order in corners of the earth that would otherwise be left to their unhappy fates.

To create an alternative institution in competition with it, such as Hoffmann's Association of Democratic Nations, Daalder and Lindsay's Alliance of Democracies, or even or the actual Community of Democracies founded by more than100 nations in 2000, would only complicate matters. Each member of the new institution, if it stayed in the UN as well, would face a constant tension between its competing obligations to both organizations. A conflict, perhaps even a direct clash between a coalition of democracies and the Security Council itself (as would have happened over Kosovo had the matter gone before the UN) would sooner or later be inevitable. Any state joining a new organization would in effect be redefining the original Charter and their obligations to it by default, placing themselves and the remaining UN loyalists on a collision course.

How, then, can the contradictions of the UN be reconciled so that it can function effectively as an instrument that can instill fear and caution in—and if need be, act against—genocidal dictators, aggressive rogues, and suicidal terrorists in an age of preventive violence? Strict interpreta-

tions of international law and of the Charter no longer have much force
or appeal, if they ever did.[45] Worse, attempts to corral violence under a
legalistic UN regime will only increase the tendency for states and their
leaders to think in terms of their own security and values rather than
loyalty to a universal institution, a "perverse effect," as Glennon calls it,
of the "effort to force a legalist use-of-force system on a world that is not
ready for it."[46]

The reason the world is not ready for a universalist legal order regarding the use of force is that the world is not populated by universally legalist regimes, and that realization points to a difficult, even radical answer
to the problem of reforming the United Nations.

A Security Council Worth Fighting for: The Case for Liberal Democratic Exceptionalism

There has been considerable debate in recent years over the question of
whether democracies are inherently less aggressive (at least against each
other) than other kinds of regimes. Whether spreading democracy can
stop terrorism or bring international peace is not the issue here; the
more important question, given the obstinacy of the dictatorships when
it comes to efforts to keep a just and humane peace among nations, is
whether terrorism, genocide, and other such threats can be stopped by
anything *but* democracies. While the democracies have much to answer
for, the record of recent history nonetheless confirms that illiberal
regimes cannot be counted on to act against threats to a liberal order.
Despite the often ludicrous, childish brawling among the democracies,
they are the best hope for defending such an order. The General Assembly will always exist, and will always need to exist, as a forum in which
even the most hideous regimes must have their say. But as the age of
prevention approaches, the Security Council must begin to function as
a genuine locus of international security in more than name only.
Accordingly, the membership and the procedures of the Security Council must be changed.

The conceptual foundation of any sensible reform of the United
Nations would consist of jettisoning years of hypocrisy and embracing
liberal democratic exceptionalism. This means going beyond utilitarian
arguments about the inherent peacefulness of democracies, and defending instead a general principle that liberal democracies—and the
qualification of *liberal* is key—are fundamentally better systems of gov-

ernment that by moral right are empowered to make decisions for the sake of the international community that despotisms may not. Explicitly establishing this principle would codify what historian Marc Trachtenberg identified over a decade ago as a "long-term historical trend . . . toward increasing recognition of *the right of the civilized world* to uphold certain standards of behavior—that states, for example, should not be free to massacre their own citizens or allow their territory to serve as a base for piracy or terrorism" (emphasis added).[47] What this would mean in practice is that regimes chosen by, and accountable to, their own people, and who seek to uphold principles such as those of the UN's own Declaration of Human Rights, have privileges in the international system that other kinds of regimes do not. No longer would a Canada or Norway or Japan have to justify itself to a Cuba or Burma or Iran, a situation that has long defied common sense and offends even a rudimentary sense of justice.

Again, this is not an argument for the superiority of democracies, if "democracy" is denoted merely as a political system in which majorities rule by voting. There are places in the world where majorities of people choose illiberal leaders and cheer them on as they call for tearing down the liberal order and its principles. The mere presence of elections might mean that Venezuela and even Iran could count as "democratic," even as their leaders tussle with their own populations in trying to repress dissident groups and mangle the system that got them elected in the first place. They have no place in a body trying to establish and maintain a just international order.

Nor is this an argument that the liberal democracies will overall be more pacifistic than other kind of regimes. As Michael Doyle has pointed out, liberal democratic states go to war, too, but they do so more cautiously. Moreover, because their leaders are accountable to their people and their states are founded on liberal ideas, liberal democracies tend to fight for liberal purposes. This, Doyle notes, "does not produce peace. The historical liberal legacy is laden with popular wars fought to promote freedom, protect private property or support liberal allies against nonliberal enemies."[48] The idea is not that liberal regimes will take up arms less often, but only that they are more likely than other kinds of governments to take them up for reasons of right and justice.

But how would this liberal democratic exceptionalism be enforced at the United Nations, and how would it help to keep an age of prevention from turning to an age of chaos?

The structural expression of this affirmation of the supremacy of liberal democracy would be to close the membership of the Security Council to illiberal regimes. The Council would exclude states whose leaders govern by coercion, are unaccountable to their own people, and who suppress basic human freedoms. This is not some sort of Kantian demand that all states finally alter their constitutions and become republics.[49] Rather, it is a structural attempt to empower states that embrace the rule of law and the rights of free human beings, and to disempower the autocracies who would tear apart the foundations upon which institutions such as the UN are built. Membership in the General Assembly would be a right that derives from existence as a recognized state, but membership in the Security Council would be a privilege earned and maintained by a state's behavior, both internal and external.

Such a restructuring would amount to a declaration that regimes that violate human rights, threaten international order, and seek ever more lethal technologies will no longer be welcomed in deliberations about whether to use force against regimes that consistently violate human rights, threaten international order, and seek ever more lethal technologies. There is a reason that many democracies do not allow felons to vote or sit on juries, and this jurisprudential principle should now be applied in the international community as well.

While this could be derided as discriminatory, the Security Council, with its permanent and unaccountable Big Five, is already inherently and structurally discriminatory. The existence of the Security Council veto, in particular, "makes nonsensical the Charter's organizing principle of sovereign equality."[50]

Vetoing the Veto

Concurrent with this reform of the Security Council's membership, the veto as it is currently practiced should be abolished. This is not because it is an intrinsically bad idea; the Security Council veto—what Paul Kennedy calls the "sacred, encrusted veto"—is not necessarily any worse an idea than the veto of a domestic presidential system.[51] It slows intemperate action and allows the five permanent members the ability to act with less fear of being overtaken by resolutions of hostile intent. But it is an *absolute* veto, with no hope of overturning it. This vests too much power in a single nation, no matter who it is; as Canadian scholar Brecher argues, in an age of rogues and terrorists, "decisions on war and peace are too important to be left to the whims, threats, or machinations of any single member-state."[52]

Even in 1945, there were concerns about the veto and there were already proposals to undermine it, as two American historians later wrote:

> State Department planners proposed that the Big Four [the U.S., UK, USSR, and Nationalist China] veto should not be absolute, but they drew an odd distinction between two kinds of situations: decisions involving "peaceful settlement" of disputes should require a two-thirds affirmative vote, including all of the Big Four; and decisions involving the use of force to suppress aggression should also require a two-thirds affirmative vote, but only three of the Big Four. The latter formulation meant that a permanent member could not use the veto to prevent a Security Council [resolution] it opposed, including action against itself.[53]

This restriction was, of course, later rejected by all the Big Four, and it would have been surprising had any of its founders accepted such limitations. But it is telling that even at the moment of creation, there was some sense that the very powers that were supposed to keep the peace might in fact themselves be the obstacles to that same peace.

If the Council were restructured to admit only liberal regimes, perhaps by vote of established democracies who mutually recognize and accept each other as such, then it should be possible to create a mechanism by which a supermajority of the Council could defeat the veto of one member. This would be a way out of the paralysis in which the Council constantly finds itself, and could open the way for greater agreement, if at the cost of unanimity (which is rarely attainable anyway) in Council decisions.[54] In turn, powerful democracies, including the United States, might be more inclined to think of the United Nations as the first resort in times of danger, since the Security Council's decisions would be the product of deliberation among states like themselves that they would, at least theoretically, be more likely to trust. No great power will ever abide by a decision it finds utterly unacceptable, but where there is room for compromise, the moral force of a preponderance of voting democracies might have more influence than a five-way chess game among the veto-holders, two of whom are, to put it mildly, ambiguous about the rights of free human beings. While there may always be conflicts with prickly powers like France, disagreements between France and the United States are at least arguments between allies who have both sacrificed the lives of their sons and daughters for the defense of liberty, and have thus earned a greater right to decide questions of international order than thuggish states like Syria or North Korea whose leaders have spent human life mostly to keep themselves in power and their people oppressed.

This is also a solution that finally opens the door to genuine participation by the smaller powers. UN official Tharoor has complained about the "unseemly sneering over the right of Angola, Cameroon, or Guinea to pass judgment in the [Security Council]," which "overlooks the valuable contribution their presence makes."[55] The great powers, however, might well sneer at diatribes and demands in the Council by tiny states because they know that the nations involved will have no say in the outcome, and will not be risking the lives of their citizens if the outcome is war. But a Security Council in which the larger powers might have to court the vote of smaller nations, particularly to overcome the veto of one of the permanent members, would dramatically increase the importance and relevance of smaller members.[56] Gilles Andréani sees the United Nations as a place where even the most difficult nations can be "socialized," and what better socialization than to be a member of the Security Council with a vote that actually might matter?[57]

Here, the United States will have to exercise the boldest kind of leadership. A stated American willingness to abide by such a reformed veto would create palpable pressure on other states to follow suit, not only because it would represent Washington's stunning departure from sixty years of precedent, but because it would show an American willingness to accept new rules that could actually constrain the use of U.S. power.

Of course, any radical proposal for reform is unlikely to succeed because of the tautology of the veto: changes in the nature of the Council and the veto will be, of course, vetoed. But change is possible if the United States and the major powers of the world agree that the original Charter is outdated—as Australia, for one, has been suggesting—and then threaten unilaterally to revise their own understanding of the Charter and their right to self-defense if their demands are not met.

That is, the U.S. and others advocating reforms would have to demand that the UN change, or henceforth issues of international security will be settled in councils held outside of New York. America and other like-minded nations might retain their membership in the UN, but they would now refuse even to go through the motions of submitting proposed military action to the Security Council for approval.

The democratic great powers, if stymied by a Security Council that refuses to change, would leave Turtle Bay (taking their checkbooks with them), and make their own arrangements. UN bureaucrats would be left only to supervise things like literacy programs and child vaccinations on whatever budget wealthier states wish to afford them. It is an unpalatable alternative, but one no worse either than the emergence of competing organizations to supplant the UN or the complete anarchy of unrestrained unilateralism.

Among the many impediments to reform of the Security Council, the most obvious can be summed up in five words: *The People's Republic of China*. How can any of this take place when the world's largest dictatorship holds a permanent seat in what should be a conclave of democracies?

There is no easy answer to this. The Security Council might be one of the most ossified political bodies on earth, and that probably suits the interests of China and other autocratic states. The first step, however, to limiting China's power to oppose the democracies would be to defang the veto. If the U.S., UK, France, and even Russia were to agree to limits on the veto, this could be a development that China might see as having no choice but to accept. But like China, Russia and France exercise diplomatic power in the Council far in excess of their actual military or economic capacity only because of their absolute veto, and might even be inclined to join China in opposing a new, democratically sustained veto. (Britain, it could be argued, punches above its weight in international affairs not because of its veto, but because of its unique relationship with the United States and greater willingness to employ its military forces.) But the French and the Russians should be reminded that their systems of domestic government, like America's, contain similar veto override mechanisms, and it is possible that they might accept that their interests would be less threatened by a chamber composed only of liberal democracies whose voters would be no more volatile or emotional than their own—and whose collective voice could overcome Beijing's veto.

One optimistic sign is that China has not opposed what appears to be a recent tendency for the Security Council to act in favor of democracy, as John Owen has noted:

Is a norm arising calling for the extirpation of illiberal government wherever it is found? Such a norm, of course, would lead to continuous interventions around the world. But so long as China remains illiberal, the Security Council will not adopt that norm. Instead, it seems to have adopted a more limited norm opposing the forcible overthrow of liberal government. The Council is leaving established authoritarian States alone, but acting to restore liberal government where it has been illegally removed.[58]

China may not be opposing this trend because it seems to include a kind of "grandfather clause" for existing dictatorships. And indeed, assurances by the United States and the other democracies in a reformed UN that they will not embark on a crusade of democratization (especially in the wake of Operation Iraqi Freedom) might be necessary. But likewise, there is no reason for the democracies to accept a retroactive absolution of all current UN members when it comes to qualifying for Security Council membership, seats on committees on human rights or disarmament, or anything else.

If the other major powers insist on change, the PRC would have the choices of accepting its seat in a reformed Security Council or opting out of the United Nations system entirely. If the world's largest country leaves the UN, it could be the final blow to the Charter. But if China defects alone, it would be choosing to return to its pre-1971 status as something of a pariah state. Neither alternative is a happy one, but neither is worse than the collapse of order that will come without UN reform. If need be, better that China, or the United States, or Russia or, for that matter, any of the great powers, step away from the United Nations rather than act as hypocritical cornerstones of a illusory community that has in reality fractured into disorder, and in which dictatorships and democracies alike act only as they will and as they are able.

The potentially irresolvable problem of China aside, there are numerous other diplomatic objections which might be raised about redefining Security Council membership. On a purely practical level, the symbolism of closing the Security Council to illiberal states means offending more than a few American friends and riling regimes like Pakistan who are providing significant support—at the moment, anyway—in the struggle against terrorism. There have already been incidents that foreshadow such conflicts: Uzbekistan's president, for example, in 2005 decided he had heard enough U.S. criticism of his authoritarian ways and demanded that the Americans vacate their air base in his country. Drawing a bright line between democracies and dictatorships will be difficult to do, and risks alienating nations struggling in the transition to freedom. This kind of exceptionalism in the Security Council could end up only widening the gulf between the democracies and the countries they hope to shepherd away from the addiction of authoritarianism.

But the plain fact is that is that the United States and its major allies already practice discrimination in organizations like the G-8, NATO, and the European Union. (Just ask Russia or Turkey.) In these institutions, the democracies have taken a stand that they should take in the United Nations: that in order to join us in our discussions about administering the global economy and the global peace, you must first represent a regime whose character and values are at least something like ours. This is not a plan for turning the Security Council into some shadowy power unto itself; rather, it is a call to enhance its moral clarity and political coherence and to provide powerful incentives for nations wishing to join it to alter their behavior accordingly. Countries with a more mixed or unstable record of liberal democracy would face a choice: continue toward liberalism and remain in the organization, or backtrack toward repression and be excluded from deliberations on matters of extreme importance. This is a dilemma, for example, that critics of the increasingly illiberal regime in the Kremlin believe should be forced upon Russia regarding its membership in the G-8, and it might well be argued that Russia has not slid further back toward repression, and is not a more illiberal regime, precisely because it wants to keep its place in the G-8, just as other states would hope to maintain their right to sit in a new Security Council.

But a second answer to these charges of discrimination might be to ask: So what?

At what point do the nations who have created and sustain the liberal international order cease apologizing for insisting on the right to decide measures to protect global peace without having to consult their own enemies for permission? Or as George Shultz put it: "If you are one of these criminals in charge of a state, you no longer should expect to be allowed to be inside the system at the same time that you are a deadly enemy of it."[59] What possible sense could it make to ask those who by definition oppose the status quo also to defend it—and then to accept their inevitable refusal as binding on everyone else?

None of this is to deny the historical sins, blunders, and even crimes that the democracies have committed in the past century in establishing the international system as it exists today. But acknowledging, for example, that Belgium and Japan were once cruel colonial powers does not logically lead to the conclusion that they therefore and in perpetuity, no matter what atonement they make or how much they change, have no better moral right to intervene against *génocidaires* or to destroy terrorist training camps than the countries that actually produce or support such threats.

Moreover, when states fail, when they plunge into the bloody free-fall of complete disorder and become dangers to others, who should rescue and then administer them? Should dictators and warlords be consulted about how best to quell situations that they themselves might have created, or that they see as in their interest? Paul Kennedy argues that concepts like the UN Trusteeship Council, or even the "mere mention" of it, "infuriates countries that were not sovereign in 1945 and remain sensitive to any hint of covert Western colonialism and patronizing," thus making any revival of trusteeships "politically impossible."[60] But why should this be so? The lives of millions cannot be held hostage to political correctness. Does the imperialist history of the developed world mean that its nations are now forever barred from helping people in need, or that there is no difference between soldiers wearing the blue flag of the United Nations and those who once wore the insignia of some long-defunct empire? Certainly, preventive or humanitarian interventions should not be the pretext for ensuring the hegemony of a small circle of powers by crushing all challenges to the status quo. But hypothetical fears of neo-imperialism should likewise not be the argument for inaction in the face of very real and tangible dangers.

In the end, such objections might well soon be moot, because they are already being overtaken by events. The wars in Iraq and Afghanistan, and their subsequent occupations, were in fact actions taken by coalitions of democracies in order to topple terrible governments and place their populations under de facto trusteeships until elections could be held to create freely chosen, if not yet completely independent, governments in both of them. In Afghanistan, the United States issued an ultimatum to a neanderthalic regime that was not recognized by the rest of the world (save for Pakistan, which created it), and when the ultimatum expired, the regime was removed and the country put under the administration of a multinational force. In Iraq, the U.S., the UK, and their allies made a calculation that the regime in Baghdad had finally become an intolerable threat—to say nothing of being a painful affront to the conscience of any decent human being—and again, after an ultimatum, they removed it by force. They have since administered the affairs of Iraq, with the U.S. coalition attempting to act, with varying degrees of competence, as the guardian of the Iraqi state until it could be handed to Iraqis chosen by their own people. Neither Iraq nor Afghanistan were ever officially called a "trusteeship" or "protectorate," but if we are to call things by their right name, that is what they were.

Critics may well object that is pure arrogance to declare certain governments incompetent or dangerous, and then to attack their territory and remove their leaders. It is easy to see where the assertion that some political systems are better than others could produce unease, irritation, and fear. But such objections are, in the main, irrelevant, as they will not stop the great powers from taking action again when they think they must. This is not a prediction of an endless series of wars of regime change, but rather a recognition that many states will continue to engage in ongoing military activity against regimes and groups they perceive as a threat, regardless of permission from the UN or anyone else. It might be better simply to abandon pretenses and accept the reality that there are states and quasi-states that either cannot, or will not, administer their own affairs in a way that is not a danger to their own people or to others. When they must be reckoned with by force, as some of them necessarily will be, such actions should be exercised within the constraints of, and as much as possible subject to, the requirements of a reformed Security Council.

Unless the iron tautology of the veto is broken and the composition of the Security Council changed in a way that reflects the growing wave of global democratization, the United Nations will be doomed, at least as any kind of recognized arbiter of the use of force. If states are going to act on notions of rights and justice in going to war, whether to alleviate suffering or to prevent aggression, terrorism, or other disasters, international organizations must be constituted by members who believe that each has at least some moral standing to levy judgment on the other or they will reject community action in favor of unilateral solutions. No matter how much unseemly hissing and catcalling may sometimes take place between the liberal democracies, there is an essential bond of trust between them that makes cooperation more possible than between liberal states and their illiberal opponents.

This kind of trust will be essential to governing the use of force in an age of prevention, because without it, the temptation to self-help will become almost irresistible, especially if the formal institutions of international order become increasingly divorced from how that order is actually maintained. Glennon has put it best in comparing the two "universes" of conflict resolution in the modern world and his description is worth considering at length:

> In one universe a *de jure* regime continues the traditional pacific dispute settlement process established by the Charter. . . . In the other universe is a *de facto* system. It is a geopolitical regime over which the strong preside. It bears little resemblance to the formal regime of the Charter. Its ordering principle is not consent but power. Its rules are made not by students' international law journals but by NATO activation orders and the Pentagon's rules of engagement. Its membership is selective. Its participants are the like-minded states of NATO and other Western democracies . . . [who] by and large trust one another because they share the same values. They support the jaw-jawing of the *de facto* regime because they recognize that when pacific dispute settlement fails, it is they who will have to do the heavy lifting: When international order is threatened . . . they are the ones to restore it.[61]

This de facto order exists is because the regimes in it realize their democratic and humanistic values cannot be served by international institutions which are infested by some of the worst enemies of democracy and humanity. It is time at least to acknowledge, if not solve, this problem.

Only the United States has the power and prestige—prestige that is for now deeply but only temporarily damaged—to lead such a self-sacrificing change in international norms. Only America can shame the other nations of the world into giving up even the smallest measure of sovereignty in the name of greater peace. And only America, with its great power and its many allies, can offer protection to those who might, however fearfully, be willing to hand their own defense to the Security Council. But so long as the Security Council remains the last bastion of an outdated notion of absolute sovereignty that serves only the interests of the very worst regimes on earth, then all the power, promises, and persuasion in the world will not head off the eventual collapse of the United Nations, the anarchy it will inevitably produce, and the consequent advent of uncontrolled preventive war.

Afterword: Now What?

> *Jimmy Malone:* You said you wanted to get Capone. Do you really wanna get him? You see what I'm saying is, what are you prepared to do?
> *Eliot Ness:* Everything within the law.
> *Malone:* And *then* what are you prepared to do?
>
> —*From* The Untouchables

There is, I realize, a sort of grimness to this book, with its long march through twenty years of civil war, genocide, and terrorism, all under the shadow of the growing certainty that at some point a terrifying chemical, biological, or nuclear attack will eventually take place in a major Western city. And there does seem to be a depressing inevitability to it: the worst threats to international security are no longer exotic technologies in the hands of nation-states. They are the ordinary conveniences that surround our lives, perverted from their useful ends into instruments of mass murder. They are as simple as jet airliners aimed at buildings or cell-phone-activated bombs on subways. And even nuclear bombs and other sophisticated weapons, made from technologies that are decades old, will soon enough be available either by purchase or manufacture to even the dimmest fanatics and the most backward states.

Terrorists are not geniuses, no more than are delusional rogue leaders or their sycophants. What they are, however, is dedicated. And so the international community now faces the frustrating question that Sean Connery's veteran cop posed in the classic film *The Untouchables* to Kevin Costner's rookie investigator, Eliot Ness, after every attempt to use the standard mechanisms of law enforcement had failed to corral the brutal king of the mobsters, Al Capone: "What are you prepared to do?"

The problem, as I have argued in this book, is that the unpredictable, rash nature of these enemies has successfully tempted the United States and many other counties to abandon traditional rules and norms about war. Perhaps some of these strictures were outdated; perhaps some of them were pages of law books that were long overdue to be torn out and discarded. But some of them were also barriers to the precipitous use of violence, and they, too have been left behind. The answer to the question of what we are prepared to do, then, is: almost anything, apparently, including striking enemies not only without being struck first, but if there is even a suspicion that they might one day pose a threat.

This may not always be as imprudent a policy as it seems, but it is a course laden with dangers both to international peace and to our own sense of ourselves in the West as the guardians of a just and law-based community of nations. And yet, I would argue there is cause for at least some optimism for the future, even with the certainty of danger ahead.

In a famous analogy, political scientist Arnold Wolfers argued many years ago that states are somewhat like people: when facing a lethal peril, like finding themselves in a house ablaze, they will all act alike.[1] They will head for the exits, grab fire extinguishers, and in general do what anyone, of any nationality or background, would do under the circumstances. The burning house represented a world at war, where states could be expected to pursue their interests and defend themselves in pretty much the same ways, seeking power and advantage, attacking their enemies, and ensuring their own security by the most coercive means at their disposal. The behavior of states at war, like people in a burning house, shows little variation. But for Wolfers, the more interesting question was what happens when people don't agree on the threat. What if the house is merely too warm, or someone claims to smell smoke? Crisis, not disaster, is what brings out the idiosyncrasies of both people and states.

The house is not yet on fire, but just about everyone smells smoke. And contrary to expectation, many nations seem to be reaching similar conclusions about how to prevent a five-alarm catastrophe. Each, in a way, has decided to form its own fire department, and each will choose when to flood the house, regardless of the other tenants.

America cannot stop this trend. But it can exercise leadership in making sure that the international order is not swept away in a torrent of competing preventive actions, all of which might be well intentioned attempts in the short term to save Wolfers's house, but in the long term will collectively destroy it as surely as any major conflagration.

The most important change the United States can make in coming years is to recommit itself to international institutions and to the United Nations above all. For many Americans—myself among them—this is a painful prospect. The United Nations easily qualifies as one of the world's most dysfunctional bureaucracies, and there is no shortage of anti-Americanism to be found in it. But American obstinacy about the United Nations must end. It is the only institution that can command any kind of support outside of the developed world, which is where force will most likely and most often have to be used.

This does not mean that the United States must passively return to the quagmire of the Security Council and argue in vain with dictatorships that have no business deciding the fate of the civilized world. An American recommitment to the United Nations must also include demands that the international community be an actual *community*, composed of likeminded and liberal states that will not tolerate thugs, madmen, and genocidal fanatics in their ranks.

This is an immense, even revolutionary, demand, and the Americans and their allies must be willing to lead by example. The United States in particular, as the strongest power on earth—actually, the strongest power ever to exist—should agree to restrain the use of American might in exchange for the protections of a common defense. This means taking multilateralism seriously. As Henry Kissinger—himself an early opponent of prevention who now accepts that it may in some cases be necessary—argues, "a policy that allows for preventive force can sustain the international system only if solitary American enterprises are the rare exception, not the basic rule of American strategy."[2] But if America is to embrace multilateralism as more than an incantation uttered in advance of the formation of ad hoc coalitions, then the Americans in turn have the right to insist that other nations, in Kissinger's words, "take the new [security] challenges seriously and to treat them as something beyond the sole responsibility of America."

The advent of an age of prevention is a potential tragedy. If we are not careful, it could well end up representing the defeat of three centuries in which nations and their leaders struggled to define laws and traditions to help us to retain some sense of humanity even in those awful moments just before we might have to decide to kill each other. But for better or worse, change has been forced on the international community by groups and states that care nothing for the price that was paid to ransom a new international order over sixty years ago. We can choose to stand together, and to act as members of the human family against threats both to peace and human rights. This might mean more rather than less conflict and violence, but at least these would be wars undertaken under a common banner of humanity. Or we can return to the ways of our ancestors, abandoning each other in a futile and bloody search for our own security.

We do not have long to decide.

Notes

Chapter 1. A New Age of Prevention

1. The Nuremberg judgment relating to this issue is online at Yale Law School's Avalon Project, http://www.yale.edu/lawweb/avalon/imt/proc/juddenma.htm.

2. William V. O'Brien, *The Conduct of Just and Limited War* (New York: Praeger, 1981), 132.

3. Stephen Krasner, "The Day After," *Foreign Policy* (January/February 2005): 68–69.

4. Interview with Maj. Gen. Peter Williams, UKAR, Moscow, April 7, 2005.

5. Lawrence Freedman, "Prevention, Not Preemption," *Washington Quarterly* 26 (2) (Spring 2003): 107.

6. O'Brien, *Conduct of Just and Limited War*, 133.

7. See, for example, Roger Coate, "The UN and the Legal Status of Preemptive and Preventive War," in Betty Glad and Chris Dolan, eds., *Striking First: Preemption and Preventive War Doctrines and the Reshaping of US Foreign Policy* (New York: Palgrave Macmillan, 2004), 169.

8. The immediate events that precipitated the war, Thucydides tells us, were merely a "pretext." Thucydides, *The Landmark Thucydides: A Comprehensive Guide to the Peloponnesian War*, ed. Robert Strasser (New York: Free Press, 1996), 65. For an account of the Spartan debates, see W. Robert Connor, *Thucydides* (Princeton, N.J.: Princeton University Press, 1984), 36–47.

9. See Marc Trachtenberg, *History and Strategy* (Princeton, N.J.: Princeton University Press, 1991), 103–4.

10. Quoted in *Trachtenberg, History and Strategy*, 106; see also Lloyd Mathews, "The Speech Rights of Air Professionals," *Airpower Journal* (Fall 1998): 22.

11. The quote has been widely cited over the past 50 years. For an original report, see "Instituting a War," *Time*, September 4, 1950, via online archive at Time.com.

12. See William Burr and Jeffrey Richelson, "Whether to 'Strangle the Baby in the Cradle'," *International Security* 25 (3) (Winter 2000/01).

13. Major Steven Prebeck, USAF, "Preventive Attack in the 1990s?" (Maxwell, Ala.: Air University Press, 1993), 3.

14. Michael Mandelbaum, *The Case for Goliath: How America Acts as the World's Government in the Twenty-First Century* (New York: Public Affairs, 2005), 60.

15. Melvyn P. Leffler, "Bush's Foreign Policy," *Foreign Policy* (September/October 2004): 23.

16. Thucydides, *Landmark Thucydides*, 352.

17. The language of the National Security Strategy is indiscriminate, and uses several terms interchangeably; Section V uses "forestall," "preempt," and "prevent" all to refer to eliminating potential threats to U.S. and allied security. National Security Strategy of the United States, Section V, http://www.whitehouse.gov/nsc/nss5.html.

18. "President Says Saddam Hussein Must Leave Iraq in 48 Hours," available at CNN at http://www.cnn.com/2003/WORLD/meast/03/17/sprj.irq.bush.transcript/.

19. Peter Dombrowski and Rodger A. Payne, "The Emerging Consensus for Preventive War," *Survival* 48 (2) (2006): 115.

20. Paul Schroeder, "Iraq: The Case Against Preemptive War," *American Conservative Magazine* online, October 2002, at http://www.amconmag.com/1021/iraq.html.

21. John Lewis Gaddis, "Grand Strategy in the Second Term," *Foreign Affairs* 84 (1) (January/February 2005): 5.

22. I was present when commentator and erstwhile presidential candidate Pat Buchanan made this latter comment during a campaign stop at Dartmouth College when he ran against George H. W. Bush for the Republican nomination in 1991.

23. Anatoly Dobrynin, *In Confidence: Moscow's Ambassador to America's Six Cold War Presidents (1962–1986)* (Seattle: University of Washington Press, 2001), 407.

Chapter 2. Humanitarian Intervention, Sovereignty, and Prevention

Epigraphs: Geremek quoted in Michael J. Glennon, *Limits of Law, Prerogatives of Power: Interventionism After Kosovo* (New York: Palgrave, 2001), 160; Office of the Prime Minister, "Prime Minister Warns of Continuing Global Terror Threat," March 5, 2004, http://www.number-10.gov.uk/output/Page5461.asp; Michael Mandelbaum, *The Case for Goliath: How America Acts as the World's Government in the Twenty-First Century* (New York: Public Affairs, 2005), 70.

1. Roméo Dallaire, *Shake Hands with the Devil: The Failure of Humanity in Rwanda* (New York: Avalon, 2003), 510.

2. See Section B of *The Responsibility to Protect: Report of the International Commission on Intervention and State Sovereignty* (Ottawa: IDRC, 2001).

3. Quoted in Samantha Power, *A Problem from Hell: America and the Age of Genocide* (New York: Perennial, 2003) 413.

4. Power, *A Problem from Hell*, 413.

5. Quoted in Nicholas Wheeler, *Saving Strangers: Humanitarian Intervention in International Society* (New York: Oxford University Press, 2003), 178.

6. Wheeler, *Saving Strangers*, 172.

7. Republican Senator Richard Lugar (R-Ind.) claimed that the "Clinton administration was not comfortable with the use of military power and simply hoped it wouldn't have to be used." Quoted in PBS, *Frontline* #1704, "Ambush

in Mogadishu," air date November 1, 2001, transcript http://www.pbs.org/wgbh/pages/frontline/shows/ambush/etc/script.html.

8. Quoted in Wheeler, *Saving Strangers*, 182.

9. There is an excellent detailed discussion of this point in Wheeler, *Saving Strangers*, 183.

10. Interview with François Heisbourg, Paris, October 19, 2006.

11. Interview in "Ambush in Mogadishu."

12. For a good summary of the various arguments on this point, see Mickey Kaus, "What *Black Hawk Down* Leaves Out," *Slate*, January 21, 2002.

13. "Ambush in Mogadishu."

14. Clinton tried explicitly to avoid the appearance of personalizing the conflict, to no avail. See Clinton's "Address to the Nation on Somalia," October 7, 1993, available at the American Presidency Project at http://www.presidency.ucsb.edu/ws/index.php?pid=47180. See also the comments of former U.S. ambassador to Somalia Robert Oakley made as part of the *Frontline* background interviews at http://www.pbs.org/wgbh/pages/frontline/shows/ambush/interviews/oakley.html.

15. Journalist Mark Bowden's book, *Black Hawk Down: A Story of Modern War* (New York: Atlantic Monthly Press, 1999) was made into a motion picture of the same name by director Ridley Scott in 2001.

16. One Army Ranger involved in the battle described it as like a huge "moving target range," finding it upsetting how "easy" it was to keep hitting people at will. "Ambush in Mogadishu."

17. "Ambush in Mogadishu."

18. "Ambush in Mogadishu."

19. Bin Laden specifically referred to the Battle of Mogadishu and how it revealed the extent of American "impotence and weakness" in his 1996 declaration of war against America, and Hussein actually distributed copies of the movie *Black Hawk Down* to his troops just prior to the 2003 invasion of Iraq as something like an instructional video on how to defeat U.S. forces. See Osama bin Laden, "Declaration of War Against the Americans Occupying the Land of the Two Holy Places," August 23, 1996, http://www.pbs.org/newshour/terrorism/international/fatwa1996.ht ml . Saddam's fascination with *Black Hawk Down* was first reported in *Time*'s March 2003 issue.

20. Power, *A Problem from Hell*, 352.

21. The shootdown of Habyarimana's plane is a mess that may never be untangled. (The black box retrieved from the crash site sat in a drawer at the UN for ten years, an oversight an embarrassed Kofi Annan called a "first class foul up.") The declassified State Department report sent the morning after the shootdown is available online at the National Security Archive, http://www.gwu.edu/%7Ensarchiv/NSAEBB/NSAEBB119/Rw4.pdf. For more on the French report, see BBC News, "Rwanda Genocide 'Failure' Berated," April 5, 2004, http://news.bbc.co.uk/1/hi/world/africa/3599493.stm, and Tim Butcher, "France Accused of Genocide by Rwanda's leader," *Daily Telegraph* online, March 17, 2004, at http://www.telegraph.co.uk/news/main.jhtml?xml=/news/2004/03/17 /wrw an17.xml&sSheet=/news/2004/03/17/ixworld.html.

22. Dallaire, *Shake Hands with the Devil*, 255.

23. Power, 366–67, 333.

24. Government of Australia, Office of the Defence Minister, "Speech by Robert Hill, the John Bray Memorial Oration," November 28, 2002, http://www .defence.gov.au/minister/HillSpeechtpl.cfm?CurrentId = 2121.

25. Christiane Amanpour, "Looking Back at Rwanda Genocide," CNN.com, April 6, 2004, http://www.cnn.com/2004/WORLD/africa/04/06/rwanda .amanpour/.

26. See http://www.cnn.com/2003/WORLD/meast/01/22/sprj.irq.wrap/.

27. See James Traub, *The Best of Intentions: Kofi Annan and the UN in the Era of American Power* (New York: Farrar, Strauss and Giroux, 2006), 186–88.

28. WSJ OpinionJournal.com, "The End of NATO," February 10, 2003, http://www.opinionjournal.com/editorial/feature.html?id = 110003049

29. Where this term originated is questionable; examples of the word "cleansing" can be found in Eastern Europe before 1941, but it is difficult to distinguish such statements from outright genocidal policies. The term entered the Western media widely in the early 1990s with reference to the Yugoslav situation.

30. Serb rapists would taunt their victims about being impregnated with Serb babies—or "little Chetniks," or "Serb soldiers"—and would sometimes hold them while pregnant for several months until abortion was impossible. See Beverly Allen, *Rape Warfare: The Hidden Genocide in Bosnia-Herzegovina and Croatia* (Minneapolis: University of Minnesota Press, 1996), 62–86.

31. See John R. Schindler, *Unholy Terror: Bosnia, al-Qa'ida, and the Rise of Global Jihad* (St. Paul, Minn: Zenith Press, 2007), chap. 8. I am grateful to Dr. Schindler for his insights on this subject.

32. Power, *A Problem from Hell*, 437.

33. Power, *A Problem from Hell*, 447

34. Stanley Hoffmann, "America Goes Backwards," *New York Review of Books*, June 12, 2003, 79.

35. Government of the United Kingdom, Prime Minister's Speeches, April 24, 1999, http://www.number-10.gov.uk/output/Page1297.asp

36. Charles Krauthammer, "The Clinton Doctrine," March 29, 1999, http:// www.cnn.com/ALLPOLITICS/time/1999/03/29/doctrine.html.

37. Wheeler, *Saving Strangers*, 267

38. Marc Trachtenberg, "Intervention in Historical Perspective," in Laura W. Reed and Carl Kaysen, eds., *Emerging Norms of Justified Intervention* (Cambridge, Mass.: American Academy of Arts and Sciences, 1993), 30.

39. This and future references to this speech are from Kofi Annan, speech to United Nations General Assembly, 54th session, September 20, 1999 (A/54/ PV.4), Official Record.

40. Michael Glennon, "Why the Security Council Failed," *Foreign Affairs* (May/June 2003).

41. François Heisbourg, "A Work in Progress: The Bush Doctrine and Its Consequences," *Washington Quarterly* (Spring 2003): 81.

42. Glennon, *Limits of Law*, 185.

43. This and future references to this article are from Gareth Evans, "The Responsibility to Protect: When It's Right to Fight," http://www.progressive-governance.net/.

44. Some legal scholars go even farther. In defending the invasion of Panama, Anthony D'Amato has argued that "human rights law" not only allows but "*demands* intervention against tyranny" (emphasis added). Anthony D'Amato, "The Invasion of Panama Was a Lawful Response to Tyranny," *American Journal of International Law* 84 (2) (April 1990).

45. Patrick Tyler and Felicity Barringer, "Annan Says U.S. Will Violate Charter if It Acts Without Approval," *New York Times*, March 11, 2003, A10.

46. Heisbourg interview.

47. Alex J. Bellamy, "Whither the Responsibility to Protect? Humanitarian Intervention and the 2005 World Summit," *Ethics and International Affairs* 20 (2) (2006): 167–68.

48. Scott Straus, "Darfur and the Genocide Debate," *Foreign Affairs* 84 (1) (January/February 2005): 131–32.

49. Anthony Clark Arend, "International Law and the Preemptive Use of Military Force," *Washington Quarterly* (Spring 2003): 101.

50. Glennon, *Limits of Law*, 177–78.

51. Quoted in James Rubin, "A Very Personal War," *Financial Times*, September 30, 2000, 9.

52. Glennon, *Limits of Law*, 209. Or, as international legal scholar W. Michael Reisman observed succinctly in 2000, "It is no longer feasible or morally acceptable to suspend the operation of human rights norms until every constitutive problem is solved." W. Michael Reisman, "Sovereignty and Human Rights in Contemporary International Law," in Gregory H. Fox and Brad R. Roth, eds., *Democratic Governance and International Law* (Cambridge: Cambridge University Press, 2000), 257.

53. Some scholars hotly dispute this. European legal scholar Bruno Simma has argued not only that humanitarian interventions without Security Council authorization are illegal, but that even the very *threat* of force might be prohibited. Furthermore, "as long as humanitarian crises do not transcend borders, as it were, and lead to armed attacks against other states, recourse to [self-defense under] Article 51 is not available." See Bruno Simma, "NATO, the UN and the Use of Force: Legal Aspects," *European Journal of International Law* 10 (1999): 5.

54. Quoted in Odd Arne Westad, "The Fall of Détente and the Turning Tides of History," in Odd Arne Westad, ed., *The Fall of Détente: Soviet-American Relations During the Carter Years* (Oslo: Scandinavian University Press, 1997), 17. For more on the failure of "linkage" during the Cold War, see Thomas M. Nichols, *Winning the World: Lessons for America's Future from the Cold War* (Westport, Conn.: Praeger, 2003), chap. 5.

55. The transcript of the debate is available from PBS at http://www.pbs.org/newshour/debatingourdestiny/84debates/2prez1.html.

56. Gilles Andréani and Pierre Hassner, "Morality and International Violence," in Andréani and Hassner, eds., *Justifier la guerre? de l'humanitaire au contre-terrorisme* (Paris : Presses de la fondation nationale des sciences politiques, 2005).

57. Lee Feinstein and Anne-Marie Slaughter, "A Duty to Prevent," *Foreign Affairs* (January/February 2004): 149–50.

Chapter 3. The End of Deterrence?

Epigraphs: William J. Perry, "Preventive Defense," speech to the Trilateral Commission, New York, May 23, 1996, http://www.trilateral.org/nagp/regmtgs/96/0523perry.htm; Lawrence Freedman, "Prevention, Not Preemption," *Washington Quarterly* 26 (2) (Spring 2003): 113.

1. George H. W. Bush, "Address to the Nation on the Commonwealth of Independent States," December 25, 1991, American Presidency Project, University of California Santa Barbara, http://www.presidency.ucsb.edu/ws/print.php?pid = 20388.

2. Richard Betts, "Suicide from Fear of Death," *Foreign Affairs* (January/February 2003): 41.

3. See, for example, Jack Snyder, *The Ideology of the Offensive: Military Decision Making and the Disasters of 1914* (Ithaca, N.Y.: Cornell University Press, 1984); Stephen Van Evera, "The Cult of the Offensive and the Origins of the First World War," *International Security* (Summer 1984).

4. Quoted in Keith Payne, *The Fallacies of Cold War Deterrence and a New Direction* (Lexington: University Press of Kentucky, 2001), 79.

5. Quoted in Payne, *Fallacies of Cold War Deterrence*, 85.

6. Payne, *Fallacies of Cold War Deterrence*, 87.

7. See Fred Kaplan, "Rumsfeld's Dr. Strangelove: Keith Payne Says 7,000 Warheads Aren't Enough," *Slate*, May 12, 2003; Colin Gray and Keith Payne, "Victory Is Possible," *Foreign Policy* (Summer 1980).

8. *Rationale and Requirements for U.S. Nuclear Forces and Arms Control*, vol, 1, *Executive Report* (Fairfax, Va.: National Institute for Public Policy, January 2001), 11.

9. William C. Martel, "Deterrence and Alternative Images of Nuclear Possession," in T. V. Paul Richard J. Harknett, and James J. Wirtz., *The Absolute Weapon Revisited: Nuclear Arms and the Emerging International Order* (Ann Arbor: University of Michigan Press, 2000), 222.

10. See Martel, "Deterrence and Alternative Images," 220; Adam Garfinkel, "Culture and Deterrence," Foreign Policy Research Institute E-Notes, August 25, 2006, www.fpri.org.

11. Lyle Goldstein, *Preventive Attack and Weapons of Mass Destruction* (Stanford, Calif.: Stanford University Press, 2006), 171.

12. There is some debate within the U.S. policy community now about the term WMD, since it includes chemical and biological weapons that, while massively lethal, are not massively destructive. A new term, "WMD/E," weapons of mass destruction/effect, seems to be coming into common usage in U.S. military and government documents.

13. See David Karl, "Proliferation, Pessimism and Emerging Nuclear Powers," *International Security* 21 (3) (Winter 1996/1997): 87.

14. Karl, "Proliferation, Pessimism and Emerging Nuclear Powers," 87.

15. Marc Trachtenberg, "Intervention in Historical Perspective," in Laura W. Reed and Carl Kaysen, eds., *Emerging Norms of Justified Intervention* (Cambridge, Mass.: American Academy of Arts and Sciences, 1993), 15.

16. John M. Deutsch, "The New Nuclear Threat," *Foreign Affairs* 71 (4) (Fall 1992): 133.

17. Michael Mandelbaum, "Lessons of the Next Nuclear War," *Foreign Affairs* 74 (2) (March/April 1995): 24.

18. Mandelbaum, "Lessons of the Next Nuclear War," 37.

19. "Interview with Ashton Carter," PBS Frontline; *Kim's Nuclear Gamble*, March 2003, http://www.pbs.org/wgbh/pages/frontline/shows/kim/interviews/acarter.html.

20. Carter, dispatched to help defuse the crisis, actually undermined Clinton's plans for sanctions, leading one Clinton cabinet member to refer to Carter as "a treasonous prick." See Chris Suellentrop, "Jimmy Carter: He Would Have Gotten Away with It if It Weren't for Those Meddling Voters," *Slate*, May 17, 2002.

21. Quoted in Robert S. Litwak, "The New Calculus of Pre-Emption," *Survival* 44 (4) (Winter 2002–2003): 56.

22. "Letter to President Clinton," available at Project for the New American Century, http://www.newamericancentury.org/iraqclintonletter.htm

23. The address was to the Pentagon and Joint Chiefs of Staff on February 17, 1998, http://www.cnn.com/ALLPOLITICS/1998/02/17/transcripts/clinton.iraq/.

24. "Transcript: President Clinton Explains Iraq Strike," December 16, 1998, http://www.cnn.com/ALLPOLITICS/stories/1998/12/16/transcripts/clinton.html

25. In a CNN appearance, Clinton told Larry King: "And then we bombed with the British for four days in 1998. We might have gotten it all; we might have gotten half of it; we might have gotten none of it. But we didn't know," transcript of *Larry King Show*, July 22, 2003, http://transcripts.cnn.com/TRANSCRIPTS/0307/22/lkl.00.html

26. Daniel Benjamin and Steven Simon, *The Age of Sacred Terror* (New York: Random House, 2002), 260.

27. Quoted in Michael Barletta, "Chemical Weapons in the Sudan: Allegations and Evidence," *Nonproliferation Review* (Fall 1998): 120.

28. Quoted in Stephen Hayes, "The Clinton View of Iraq-al Qaeda Ties," *Weekly Standard*, December 29, 2003, 16.

29. "Statement of William S. Cohen to The National Commission on Terrorist Attacks upon the United States," March 23, 2004, 10, available at 9/11 Commission website, http://www.9–11commission.gov/hearings/hearing8/cohenstatement.pdf.

30. M. Elaine Bunn, "Preemptive Action: When, How, and to What Effect?" *Strategic Forum* (U.S. National Defense University) 200 (July 2003): 2–3.

31. See, for example, the advertisement placed by several noted scholars and analysts on the op-ed page of the *New York Times*, September 26, 2002.

32. In May 2007, the *New York Times* reported that there was a "vigorous, but carefully cloaked, debate within the Bush administration" over how, or even if, terrorists and rogue states could be deterred from using nuclear terrorism against the United States or its allies. See David E. Sanger and Thom Shanker, "U.S. Debates Deterrence for Nuclear Terrorism," *New York Times*, May 8, 2007, A1.

33. Marc Weller, "The U.S., Iraq, and the Use of Force in a Unipolar World," *Survival* 41 (4) (Winter 1999–2000): 96.

34. George P. Schultz, "An Essential War," *Wall Street Journal*, March 29, 2004, 18.

35. Richard Schultz, Jr., "How Clinton Let al-Qaeda Go," *Weekly Standard*, January 19, 2004.

36. Bob Woodward, *Bush at War* (New York: Simon and Schuster, 2002), 15.

37. Woodward, *Bush at War*, 93.

38. Edgar Buckley, "Invoking Article 5," *NATO Review*, Summer 2006, http://www.nato.int/docu/review/2006/issue2/english/art2.html

39. José María Aznar, "NATO vs. Islamist Terror," *Wall Street Journal*, November 28, 2005, A16.

40. See James Mann, *Rise of the Vulcans: The History of Bush's War Cabinet* (New York: Viking, 2004), 304–5.

41. See Mann, *Rise of the Vulcans*, 304.

42. Government of the United Kingdom, "Prime Minister Warns of Continuing Global Terror Threat," http://www.number-10.gov.uk/output/Page5461.asp

43. Tomas Valasek, "Reality Check," *NATO Review* online, Summer 2006.

44. Ivo Daalder and James Goldgeier, "Global NATO" *Foreign Affairs* (September/October 2006).

45. Schultz, "How Clinton Let al-Qaeda Go," 18.

46. "Prime Minister Warns."

47. Lee Feinstein and Anne-Marie Slaughter, "A Duty to Prevent," *Foreign Affairs* (January/February 2004): 149–50.

48. Craig Gilbert, "Can U.S. Be First to Attack Enemy? After Sept. 11, Pre-Emptive Strike Should Be Option, Some Experts Argue," *Milwaukee Journal Sentinel* online, March 31, 2002.

49. Robert Lieber, "Perspectives," *E!Sharp: The Magazine of the European Union* (September-October 2006): 35.

50. Richard Posner, *Not a Suicide Pact: The Constitution in Time of National Emergency* (Oxford: Oxford University Press, 2006), 14.

51. Yehezkel Dror, *Crazy States: A Counterconventional Strategic Problem* (Millwood, N.Y.: Kraus, 1980), xvi.

52. Betts, "Suicide from Fear of Death," 41.

53. Stanley Hoffmann, "America Goes Backwards," *New York Review of Books*, June 12, 2003, 78.

54. See Lieber, "Foreign Policy 'Realists' Are Unrealistic on Iraq," *Chronicle of Higher Education*, October 18, 2002, online.

55. Daniel Byman, "Do We Understand Our Enemy?" *World Politics* 56 (October 2003): 147.

56. Quoted in William Shawcross, *Allies* (New York: Public Affairs, 2004), 13.

57. John Lewis Gaddis, "Grand Strategy in the Second Term," *Foreign Affairs* 84 (1) (January/February 2005): 2.

58. Colin Gray, "The Reformation of Deterrence," *Comparative Strategy* 22 (5) (December 2003): 441.

59. Bill Keller, "In the Long Run, Peace Can Be a Killer Too," *International Herald Tribune*, February 22, 2003.

60. Karl Mueller et al., *Striking First: Preventive and Preemptive Attack in U.S. National Security Policy* (Santa Monica, Calif.: RAND Corporation, 2006), 93.

61. Martel, "Deterrence and Alternative Images," 221.

62. "Profile: Kim Jong-Il," *BBC News World Edition* online, July 31, 2003, available at http://news.bbc.co.uk/2/hi/asia-pacific/1907197.stm.

63. For more discussion of this concept, see Anthony Clark Arend, "International Law and Rogue States: The Failure of the Charter Framework," *New England Law Review* 36 (4) (January 2003): 750.

64. Mary Ellen O'Connell, "The Myth of Preemptive Self-Defense," American Society of International Law Task Force on Terrorism, www.asil.org/taskforce/oconnell.pdf, 16n.

65. John Yoo, "International Law and the War in Iraq," *American Journal of International Law* 97 (3) (July 2003): 572.

66. Yoo, "International Law and the War in Iraq," 575.

67. Arend, "International Law and Rogue States," 750.

68. Michael Walzer, *Just and Unjust Wars*, 3rd ed. (New York: Basic Books, 2000), 74.

69. Walzer, *Just and Unjust Wars*, 81.

70. See O'Connell, "The Myth of Preemptive Self-Defense," for a detailed description of this argument.

71. O'Connell, "The Myth of Preemptive Self-Defense," 2.

72. See Yoo, "International Law and the War in Iraq," 573–74.

73. Yoo, "International Law and the War in Iraq," 574.

74. Address to the National Defense University, Washington, D.C., January 15, 1986; quoted in Michael Byers, "Letting the Exception Prove the Rule," *Ethics and International Affairs* 17 (1) (2003): 10.

75. One limitation Byers places on this is that he suggests it is only law "with respect to proven state sponsors of terrorists who have already attacked the responding state," but even that represents a significant movement in international norms over the course of a decade or so. Byers, "Letting the Exception Prove the Rule," 10, 14.

76. Ron Suskind, *The One Percent Doctrine: Deep Inside America's Pursuit of Its Enemies Since 9/11* (New York: Simon and Schuster, 2006), 32.

77. Interview with Gilles Andréani, Paris, October 20, 2006.

Chapter 4. International Perspectives on Preemption and Prevention

Epigraphs: Baluyevski quoted in Steve Gutterman, "Russia Threatens to Strike Terror Bases," AP wire, September 8, 2004; Shimada quoted in Michael Sheridan, "West Mounts 'Secret War' to Keep Nuclear North Korea in Check," *Sunday Times* online, July 9, 2006; Ivo Daalder and James Goldgeier, "Global NATO" *Foreign Affairs* (September/October 2006), online.

1. Mohamed Olad Hassan, "Ethiopian Jets Bomb Mogadishu Airport," AP wire, December 25, 2006.

2. Paul Koring, "It's Still Lose-Lose in Somalia," *Globe and Mail* online edition, December 29, 2006.

3. Elizabeth A. Kennedy, "Somalia's Islamists Vow to Heed Al-Qaeda," AP wire, January 5, 2007.

4. "Why Somalia War Unsettles the World," *Christian Science Monitor* online edition, December 29, 2006.

5. U.S. forces quickly joined the fray, attacking suspected terror targets in Somalia in early 2007.

6. Quoted in John Allen, "Vatican Shifts on Preventive War," *National Catholic Reporter,* January 23, 2004, 7.

7. George W. Bush, The National Security Strategy of the United States, 2002, http://www.whitehouse.gov/nsc/nss.html.

8. M. Elaine Bunn, "Preemptive Action: When, How, and to What Effect?" *Strategic Forum* (U.S. National Defense University) 200 (July 2003): 1. Elsewhere I have argued that preemption and prevention are not quite as new in American thinking as they have been portrayed. See Thomas Nichols, "How Really New Is the New Bush National Security Strategy?" History News Network, October 14, 2002, http://hnn.us/articles/1031.html.

9. American foreign policy analyst Robert Litwak wondered, "Could unilateral and pre-emptive military action by the United States in the post-11 September era erode international norms governing the use of force?" Robert S. Litwak, "The New Calculus of Pre-Emption," *Survival* 44 (4) (Winter 2002–2003): 53.

10. G. John Ikenberry, "America's Imperial Ambition," *Foreign Affairs* (September/October 2002): 45.

11. Peter Dombrowski and Rodger A. Payne, "Global Debate and the Limits of the Bush Doctrine," *International Studies Perspectives* 4 (2003): 406.

12. Paul Schroeder, "Iraq: The Case Against Preemptive War," *American Conservative Magazine*, October 2002, http://www.amconmag.com/1021/iraq.html.

13. Gu Guoliang, "Redefine Cooperative Security, Not Preemption," *Washington Quarterly* (Spring 2003): 138.

14. Ivo H. Daalder, James M. Lindsay, and James B. Steinberg, "The Bush National Security Strategy: An Evaluation," Brookings Policy Brief #109, October 2002, available at http://www.brookings.edu/comm/policybriefs/pb109.htm.

15. Quoted in Daalder et al., "The Bush National Security Strategy."

16. I am grateful to Dr. Bacevich for his comments on this point.

17. Stanley Hoffmann, "America Goes Backwards," *New York Review of Books,* June 12, 2003, 78.

18. Hurst Hannum, "Bellum Americanum," *Fletcher Forum of World Affairs* 27 (1) (Winter/Spring 2003): 33.

19. See Daalder et al., "The Bush National Security Strategy."

20. Melvyn P. Leffler, "Bush's Foreign Policy," *Foreign Policy* (September/ October 2004): 24.

21. Dombrowski and Payne, "Global Debate and the Limits of the Bush Doctrine," 14.

22. Tomas Valasek, "New Threats, New Rules: Revising the Law of War," *World Policy Journal* 20 (1) (Spring 2003): 20.

23. Interview with François Heisbourg, Paris, October 19, 2006.

24. "Latest al-Qaeda Tape Made France a Target: Report," Reuters wire, September 14, 2006.

25. See Jeffrey Gedmin, "Der Terror Ist Da," *Weekly Standard,* September 11, 2006.

26. "The Plan to Behead the Prime Minister," *Economist* online, June 8, 2006.

27. Lars Bevenger, "Norway Shocked by 'al-Qaeda' Threat," BBC News online, May 21, 2003.

28. Interview with Dana Allin, London, October 16, 2006.

29. Heisbourg, interview.

30. François Heisbourg, "A Work in Progress: The Bush Doctrine and its Consquences," *Washington Quarterly* (Spring 2003): 83; interview.

31. Such operations remain controversial even in a country that feels itself as threatened as Israel: there are still pitched debates about when and how such killings may be conducted. For a detailed discussion of one such debate, see Laura Blumenfeld, "In Israel, a Divisive Struggle over Targeted Killing," *Washington Post,* August 27, 2006, A1.

32. Quoted in Lucien Vandenbroucke, "The Israeli Strike Against Osiraq," *Air University Review* (September–October 1984), http://www.airpower.maxwell .af.mil/airchronicles/aureview/1984/se p -oct/vanden#vanden

33. "As the Imam said, Israel must be wiped off the map," Ahmadinejad said in late 2005, referring to Iran's revolutionary leader, the Ayatollah Khomeini. Nazila Fathi, "Wipe Israel 'off the Map' Iranian says," *International Herald Tribune* online, October 27, 2005. For the comments of the Israeli prime minister, see Yaakov Katz, "PM: Time for UN to sanction Iran," *Jerusalem Post* online (jpost.-com), December 9, 2006.

34. Heisbourg, interview.

35. Al Kamen, "The Other Right Hand," *Washington Post,* January 21, 2005, A15.

36. "Leader of Chechen Raid Expresses Condolences," *New York Times* online, June 27, 1995.

37. For a concise explanation of this theory from an experienced journalist and Russia-watcher, see David Satter, "The Shadow of Ryazan," *National Review Online,* April 30, 2002.

38. Euan Stretch, "They Knifed Babies, They Raped Girls," *Daily Mirror* online, September 5, 2004.

39. Charles Gurin, "Poll Shows Almost Half Oppose Appointing Russian Governors," *Eurasia Daily Monitor* online I (92), September 24, 2004.

40. Sophie Lambroschini, "Russia: Moscow Struggles to Clarify Stance on Preemptive Force," Radio Free Europe/Radio Liberty report, October 14, 2003.

41. Quoted in Pavel Felgenhauer, "Military Doctrine or Election Manifesto? The Ivanov Doctrine," *Perspectives* 14 (2) (January–February 2004): 1.

42. Felgenhauer, "Military Doctrine or Election Manifesto?" 1, 4.

43. See Jakub M. Godzimirski, "Russia's New Military Doctrine?" *Shortinfo from DNAK* 8/2003, http://www.atlanterhavskomiteen.no/Publikasjoner/Kort Info/Arkiv/2003/pdf/kortinfo8–2003.pdf.

44. Svetlana Babaeva, "Rossiia vpervye ob'iavila o vozmozhnosti primenenie voennoi sily protiv respublik byvshego Soiuza," *Izvestiia*, October 12, 2003.

45. Dmitri Trenin, "Russia and Global Security Norms," *Washington Quarterly* 27 (2) (Spring 2004): 68–69.

46. Quoted in Lambroschini, "Moscow Struggles."

47. Aleksandr Fedorov, ed., "Megaterrorism: A New Challenge for a New Century," *Yaderny Kontrol* Digest 8 (3–4) (Summer/Fall 2003): 33, 38–39.

48. Andrei Piontkovskii, "The Pillars of International Security: Traditions Challenged," *Yaderny Kontrol* Digest 8 (3–4) (Summer/Fall 2003): 23.

49. Piontkovskii, "Pillars of International Security," 23–24.

50. Steve Gutterman, "Russia Threatens to Strike Terror Bases," AP wire, September 8, 2004.

51. CNN.com, "Russia considers terror strikes," September 17, 2004, http://edition.cnn.com/2004/WORLD/europe/09/17/russia.putin/.

52. Interviews with Igor Neverov and Vladimir Ulianov, Russian Ministry of Foreign Affairs, and Gen. Vladimir Nikishin, Russian Ministry of Defense, Moscow, April 5–6, 2005.

53. Russian Federation Ministry of Foreign Affairs, "Kommentarii Departmenta informatsii i pechati MID Rossii v sviazi s voprosom rossiskikh CMI otnositel'no vozmozhnosti naneseniia preventivnykh udarov po bazam terroristov," ("Comment of the Department of Press Information of the MFA of Russia in response to the question from the Russian media related to the possibility of carrying out preventive strikes on terrorist bases"), February 3, 2005.

54. Matthew Tempest, "Britain Facing 'Most Sustained Threat Since WWII', Says Reid," *Guardian Unlimited*, August 9, 2006, online, http://politics.guardian.co.uk/terrorism/story/0,1840482,00.html

55. This 2003 statement is quoted in Blair's 2004 press conference; see Office of the Prime Minister, "Prime Minister Warns of Continuing Global Terror Threat," March 5, 2004, http://www.number-10.gov.uk/output/Page5461.asp.

56. Blair, "Prime Minister Warns . . ."

57. Gerard Baker, "The London Effect," *Weekly Standard*, July 25, 2005, 10.

58. Julian Glover, "British Believe Bush Is More Dangerous Than Kim Jong-il," *Guardian* online, November 3, 2006.

59. Valasek, "New Threats, New Rules," 14.

60. This and all excerpts from Government of France, Ministry of Defense, 2003–2008 Military Program, http://www.defense.gouv.fr/english/files/d140/.

61. Elizabeth Bryant, "Paris Denies Ending Deterrence Strategy," UPI wire, October 27, 2003.

62. Interview with Philippe Errera, Paris, October 20, 2006.

63. Heisbourg, interview.

64. Heisbourg, interview.

65. Heisbourg, interview; Andreani, interview.

66. Dana Priest, "Help from France Key in Covert Operations," *Washington Post*, July 3, 2005, 1.

67. Errera, interview.

68. See Dombrowski and Payne, "Global Debate and the Limits of the Bush Doctrine," for more detailed discussion of the results of the EU along these lines during its meeting on security in Greece in 2004.

69. This and following citations from European Union, "Basic Principles for an EU Strategy Against Proliferation of Weapons of Mass Destruction," June 16, 2003, http://europa-eu-un.org.

70. Anne Deighton, "Foreign Policy and European Union's Security Strategy, in Anne Deighton, ed., *Securing Europe? Implementing the European Security Strategy* (Zurich: Center for Security Studies, 2006), 28.

71. *A Secure Europe in a Better World* (Brussels: European Union, 2003), 11, and interview with Robert Cooper, Brussels, October 20, 2006.

72. This and following data taken from German Marshall Fund, *Transatlantic Trends*, 2004, 2005 2006, from "key findings" and "topline data," www.transatlantictrends.org.

73. This and following excerpts of Hill's speech are from Government of Australia, Office of the Defense Minister, "Speech by Robert Hill, The John Bray Memorial Oration," November 28, 2002, http://www.defence.gov.au/minister/HillSpeechtpl.cfm?CurrentId=2121. A shorter op-ed version of the speech appeared as Robert Hill, "The UN Charter Is Outdated," *International Herald Tribune*, December 2, 2002.

74. This and following excerpts of the 2002 interview are from Government of Australia, Office of the Prime Minister, "Transcript of the Prime Minister the Hon John Howard MP Interview with Laurie Oakes," December 1, 2002, http://www.pm.gov.au/media/interview/2002/interview2015.htm.

75. Gerard Henderson, "World Order—From the Old to the New," *Australian Journal of International Affairs* 57 (3) (November 2003): 481.

76. Henderson, "World Order," 480.

77. See Michael Perry, "Sydney Nuclear Reactor Terror Plot Target," Reuters wire, November 14, 2005; "Australia's Sydney Targeted in Terrorist Plot: Police," Agence France Presse wire, January 5, 2007.

78. Michael Sheridan, "West Mounts 'Secret War' to Keep Nuclear North Korea in Check," *Sunday Times* online, July 9, 2006.

79. See Bunn, "Preemptive Action," 6, and "Japan 'Can Seek Pre-Emptive

Strike': Constitution Allows Action if Launch Imminent, Agency Chief Says," *Japan Times*, January 25, 2003, http://www.japantimes.com.

80. Quoted in Bunn, "Preemptive Action," 7.

81. "Japan Threatens Force Against N Korea," BBC News, February 14, 2003, http://news.bbc.co.uk/1/hi/world/asia-pacific/2757923.stm.

82. Eric Heginbotham and Richard J. Samuels, "Japan's Dual Hedge," *Foreign Affairs* online author update, March 2003, http://www.foreignaffairs.org.

83. Rajan Menon, "The End of Alliances," *World Policy Journal* 20 (2) (Summer 2003): 13.

84. Mari Yamaguchi, "Japan Considers Strike Against N. Korea," AP wire, July 10, 2006.

85. Quoted in "The First Strike Option," *Asahi Shimbun—International Herald Tribune* online, July 12, 2006.

86. Quoted in *Asahi Shimbun* evening edition, July 27, 2006, 3.

87. Quoted in "Missile Tests Stir Up Debate on First-Strike Option," *Asahi Shimbun—International Herald Tribune* online, July 11, 2006

88. A 2006 *Asahi Shimbun* editorial noted that "Actually, Japan has refrained from acquiring an ability to attack enemy bases, restricting the roles and equipment of the SDF to defensive operations." See "Missile Tests Stir Up Debate." I am also grateful to Robert Dujarric for his insights on this issue.

89. As Michael Glennon has pointed out, opposition to Kofi Annan's post-Kosovo call for a new norm of intervention was most strongly resisted by Latin American, African, and Arab states—in other words, by the most authoritarian members of the UN. See Glennon, "Why the Security Council Failed," *Foreign Affairs* (May/June 2003).

90. Denny Roy, "China and the War on Terrorism," *Orbis* (Summer 2002): 517.

91. Roy, "China and the War on Terrorism," 517.

92. Quoted in Roy, "China and the War on Terrorism," 518.

93. Bates Gill and James Reilly, "Sovereignty, Intervention, and Peacekeeping: The View from Beijing," *Survival* 42 (3) (Autumn 2000): 47.

94. Chu Shulong, "China, Asia and Issues of Sovereignty and Intervention," Pugwash Occasional Papers (2) 1, January 2001, http://www.pugwash.org/reports.

95. Roy, "China and the War on Terrorism," 517.

96. See Mohan Malik, "Dragon on Terrorism: Assessing China's Tactical Gains and Strategic Losses Post-September 11" (Carlisle, Pa.: U.S Army Strategic Studies Institute, October 2002), 15.

97. Malik, "Dragon on Terrorism," 15, 22.

98. Quoted in Antoaneta Bezlova, "China's Iraq Stance Pleases US—For Now," *Asia Times Online*, October 10, 2002, http://www.atimes.com/atimes/China/DJ10Ad06.html.

99. Anne Wu, "What China Whispers to North Korea," *Washington Quarterly* 28 (2) (Spring 2005): 38, 41.

100. Cooper, interview.

Chapter 5. After Iraq

Epigraphs: Van Scherpenberg quoted in Howard LaFranchi, "Doubt Grows over Preventive War," *Christian Science Monitor*, February 4, 2004, http://www .csmonitor.com/2004/0204/p01s02-usfp.html; David C. Hendrickson and Robert W. Tucker, "A Test of Power," *National Interest* 85 (September/October 2006), online.

1. Interview with Philippe Errera, Paris, October 20, 2006.

2. Bremer made the comment during the PBS *Frontline* documentary "The Lost Year in Iraq," interview text http://www.pbs.org/wgbh/pages/frontline/yeariniraq/intervi ew s/bremer.html#4.

3. See Stephen Hayes, "The Visionary," *Weekly Standard*, May 9, 2005.

4. The high disapproval rate was in a January 2007 *Newsweek* poll. All data can be found at PollingReport.com, an online compendium of various major polls, http://www.pollingreport.com/iraq.htm.

5. "Minister Attacks 'Iraq Mistake'," BBC News online, November 17, 2006.

6. Robert J. Lieber, *The American Era: Power and Strategy for the 21st Century* (Cambridge: Cambridge University Press, 2007), vii.

7. American scholar James Carafano, for example, has pointed out that no one could have guessed that American defeat in the Vietnam war would lead the Soviet Union to believe in its own invulnerability and thus to overextend its own empire, perhaps even fatally: "The irony is our defeat in Vietnam contributed to our victory in the Cold War," quoted in Ron Hutcheson, "America's Last 'Long War' Offers Lessons for Iraq, Experts Say," Knight Ridder wire, January 21, 2007.

8. See Jonathan Schell, "The Empire Backfires," *The Nation*, March 29, 2004, 11; David Brooks, "The Iraq Syndrome, R.I.P.," *New York Times*, February 1, 2007, A23.

9. Interview with Robert Cooper, Brussels, October 20, 2006.

10. Bob Woodward, *State of Denial: Bush at War, Part III* (New York: Simon and Schuster, 2006), 488.

11. Woodward, *State of Denial*, 489.

12. Quoted in David Rose, "Neo-Culpa," *Vanity Fair*, January 2007, 85.

13. Rose, "Neo-Culpa," 82. It should be noted that several of those interviewed by Rose, with the exception of Adelman, later objected to the fact that *Vanity Fair* ran the story on its website, contrary to promises from its editors, just before the November 2006 mid-term elections. A few claimed their comments were taken out of context, but most stood by their words, complaining mostly about the story's timing, rather than its content. The symposium where several of the interviewees blasted *Vanity Fair* can be found at "*Vanity* Unfair," *National Review Online*, November 5, 2006.

14. Quoted in Rose, "Neo-Culpa," 86.

15. Peter Baker, "Embittered Insiders Turn Against Bush," *Washington Post*, November 19, 2006, A16.

16. Quoted in Rose, "Neo-Culpa," 85.

17. Baker, "Embittered Insiders Turn Against Bush," A16; see also "End of the Affair," *New Yorker*, posted online November 13, 2006.

18. Quoted in Rose, "Neo-Culpa," 86.

19. Quoted in Rose, "Neo-Culpa," 85.

20. Quoted in Baker, "Embittered Insiders Turn Against Bush," A16.

21. Quoted in Baker, "Embittered Insiders Turn Against Bush," A16.

22. Michael Glennon, "Why the Security Council Failed," *Foreign Affairs* (May/June 2003), online.

23. James Traub, *The Best of Intentions: Kofi Annan and the UN in the Era of American Power* (New York: Farrar, Strauss and Giroux, 2006), 187.

24. Woolsey told Rose, "As of mid-October of '06, the outcome isn't clear yet"; quoted in Rose, "Neo-Culpa," 85.

25. Quoted in Rose, "Neo-Culpa," 86.

26. Quoted in Rose, "Neo-Culpa," 146.

27. See Ali Akbar Dareini, "Ahmadinejad's Opponents Win in Iran Elections," Associated Press wire, December 19, 2006.

28. Dafna Linzer, "Iran Is Judged 10 Years from Nuclear Bomb: U.S. Intelligence Review Contrasts with Administration Statements," *Washington Post*, August 2, 2005, A1.

29. See, for example, Howard LaFranchi, "Doubt Grows over Preventive War," *Christian Science Monitor*, February 4, 2004.

30. Francis Fukuyama, "The Bush Doctrine, Before and After," *Financial Express*, online edition, October 17, 2005; the book is *America at the Crossroads: Democracy, Power, and the Neoconservative Legacy* (New Haven, Conn.: Yale University Press, 2006).

31. Nicholas Eberstadt, "North Korea's Weapons Quest," *National Interest* 80 (Summer 2005): 51.

32. Graham Allison, "How to Stop Nuclear Terror," *Foreign Affairs* (January/February 2004): 73.

33. Ashton Carter and William Perry, "If Necessary, Strike and Destroy," *Washington Post*, June 22, 2006, A29.

34. Kori Schake, "An American Eulogy for European Defense," in Anne Deighton, ed., *Securing Europe? Implementing the European Security Strategy* (Zurich: Center for Security Studies, 2006), 106.

35. Curt Woodward, "McCain Says Iraq Could End His Career," AP wire, February 23, 2007.

36. Edwards emphasized to an Israeli audience that "ALL options must remain on the table" (emphasis original); see http://www.herzliyaconference.org/Eng/ for original transcript. For al-Jazeera's comments, see "Senator John Edwards Pledges Before Israeli Leaders Not to Allow Iran to Have Nuclear Weapons," http://www.aljazeerah.info, January 25, 2007; Ari Berman, "Edwards's Iran Problem," *The Nation* online, "Blog: The Notion," January 29, 2007.

37. Romney needled Clinton and Clinton shot back in a February 2007 exchange. See Alex Dominguez, "Romney Says Sen. Clinton 'Timid' on Iran," AP wire, February 2, 2007.

38. John Lewis Gaddis, "Grand Strategy in the Second Term," *Foreign Affairs* 84 (1) (January/February 2005): 2.

39. Lieber, *American Era*, 229.

40. Michael Eisenstadt, "Understanding Saddam," *National Interest* 81 (Fall 2005): 119.

41. Errera, interview.

42. "Transcript: David Kay on 'Fox News Sunday'," February 1, 2004, http://www.foxnews.com/story/0,2933,110091,00.html.

43. William Shawcross, *Allies: The U.S., Britain, and Europe, and the War in Iraq* (New York: Public Affairs, 2004), 222.

44. German Marshall Fund, *Transatlantic Trends 2004: Key Findings*, 15, http://www.transatlantictrends.org/.

45. Pascal Boniface, "What Justifies Regime Change?" *Washington Quarterly* 26 (3) (Summer 2003): 69–71.

46. German Marshall Fund, *Transatlantic Trends 2004*, 13.

47. These data are available in the "Topline" report, but for some reason were not conveyed in the Key Findings; see 2006 Topline Data report http://www.transatlantictrends.org/.

48. The Americans warned the Yemenis that Washington would "take matters into its own hands" if Yemen was unwilling to take action against the terrorists there. Phillip Smucker, "The Intrigue Behind the Drone Strike," *Christian Science Monitor* online edition, November 12, 2002.

49. "Drones of Death," *Guardian Unlimited* online, November 6, 2002.

50. See Chris Downes, "'Targeted Killings' in an Age of Terror: The Legality of the Yemen Strike," *Journal of Conflict and Security Law* 9 (2) (Summer 2004).

51. Stephen Krasner, "The Day After," *Foreign Policy* (January/February 2005): 68–69.

52. Samantha Power, *The Problem from Hell: America and the Age of Genocide* (New York: Perennial, 2003), 350.

53. See Alan J. Kupferman, "Rwanda in Retrospect," *Foreign Affairs* 79 (1) (January/February 2000): 113.

54. Martha Finnemore, *The Purpose of Intervention: Changing Beliefs About the Use of Force* (Ithaca, N.Y.: Cornell University Press, 2003), 8.

Chapter 6. Governing the New Age of Prevention

Epigraphs: Robert Skidelsky, "The Just War Tradition," *Prospect*, December 2004, 31; Martin Wolf, "The United Nations," *Foreign Policy* (March/April 2007): 48.

1. David Ignatius, "We Need a New Deterrent," *Washington Post*, October 11, 2006, A19.

2. Skidelsky, "The Just War Tradition," 31.

3. Skidelsky, "The Just War Tradition," 31; Stanley Hoffmann, *World Disorders: Troubled Peace in the Post-Cold War Era* (Lanham, Md.: Rowman and Littlefield, 1998), 185.

4. Walter Russell Mead, *Power, Terror, Peace, and War: America's Grand Strategy in a World at Risk* (New York: Knopf, 2004), 65–68.

5. Mead, *Power, Terror, Peace, and War*, 67.

6. Rupert Smith, *The Utility of Force: The Art of War in the Modern World* (London: Penguin, 2005), 1.

7. Henry Kissinger, "The Rules on Preventive Force," *Washington Post*, April 9, 2006, B7.

8. Interview with Dr. John Johnson-Freese, Newport, R.I., March 23, 2007.

9. Gates got chuckles from an audience at a security conference in Munich when he said: "As an old Cold Warrior, one of yesterday's speeches," Putin's, "almost filled me with nostalgia for a less complex time. Almost." Lolita C. Baldor, "Gates to Putin: 'One Cold War Is Enough'," *ABC News* online, February 10, 2007.

10. See Thomas Nichols, "A New Cold War? Not Quite," *Toronto Star*, op-ed, May 11, 2006.

11. Irving Brecher, "In Defence of Preventive War: A Canadian's Perspective," *International Journal* (Summer 2003): 258–59.

12. Mark Steyn, "The Wisdom of George Soros's Tenant," *National Review*, July 3, 2006, 60.

13. Andrei Piontkovsky, "The Pillars of International Security: Traditions Challenged," *Yaderny Kontrol* Digest 8 (3–4) (Summer/Fall 2003): 24.

14. Gareth Evans, "The Responsibility to Protect: when it's right to fight," http://www.progressive-governance.net/."

15. Wolf, "The United Nations," 48.

16. Anthony Clark Arend, "International Law and the Preemptive Use of Military Force,"
Washington Quarterly (Spring 2003): 101.

17. Interview with Robert Cooper, Brussels, October 20, 2006.

18. Mark Steyn, "America and the United Nations," *Imprimis* 35 (2) (February 2006): 5.

19. Steyn, "America and the United Nations," 2.

20. James Traub, *The Best of Intentions: Kofi Annan and the UN in the Era of American Power* (New York: Farrar, Strauss and Giroux, 2006), 399.

21. Michael Byers, "Letting the Exception Prove the Rule," *Ethics and International Affairs* 17 (1) (2003): 15.

22. Paul M. Kennedy, *The Parliament of Man: The Past, Present, and Future of the United Nations* (New York: Random House, 2006), 250–51.

23. Mead (*Power, Terror, Peace, and War*, 202) even suggests widening the veto to nine more countries for a total of fourteen; while this might improve the Council's perceived legitimacy, how it solves the gridlock problem is unclear, at least to me.

24. As Barry O'Neill has pointed out, for example, without more veto-holding states, increasing membership in the Security Council is pointless: "as far as voting is concerned, the Security Council has five members." Indeed, increasing membership would further dilute the power of non-veto members; "their absolute power is so small, before and after, that they change makes little real differ-

ence." Barry O'Neill, "Power and Satisfaction in the Security Council," in Bruce Russett, ed., *The Once and Future Security Council* (New York: St. Martin's, 1997), 79.

25. Michael J. Glennon, "Why the Security Council Failed," *Foreign Affairs* (May/June 2003), online.

26. See Richard Roth, "Iraq to Chair U.N. Disarmament Conference," CNN.com, January 29, 2003.

27. "Blocking Reform at the U.N.," *New York Times*, December 2, 2005, A26.

28. Quoted in Robert McMahon, "Human Rights and U.N. Wrongs," *Weekly Standard*, May 23, 2005, 19.

29. Stanley Hoffmann, "America Goes Backwards," *New York Review of Books*, June 12, 2003, 79.

30. Samantha Power, *A Problem from Hell: America and the Age of Genocide* (New York: Perennial, 2003), 369.

31. Robert J. Lieber, *The American Era* (Cambridge: Cambridge University Press, 2007), 51.

32. Ian Hurd, "Of Words and Wars: The Security Council's Hard Life Among the Great Powers," *Seton Hall Journal of Diplomacy and International Relations* (Winter/Spring 2004): 70.

33. Traub, *The Best of Intentions*, 400.

34. Hoffmann, "America Goes Backwards," 80.

35. Ivo H. Daalder and James M. Lindsay, "An Alliance of Democracies," *Washington Post*, May 23, 2004, B7.

36. Andrei Piontkovskii, "The Pillars of International Security: Traditions Challenged," *Yaderny Kontrol Digest* 8 (3–4) (Summer/Fall 2003): 24.

37. Clyde Prestowitz, *Rogue Nation: American Unilateralism and the Failure of Good Intentions* (New York: Basic Books, 2003), 271.

38. Traub, *The Best of Intentions*, 173.

39. How else, Traub asks, "could they have unequivocally declared that they would not vote to authorize war, even though they had no idea whether or not Saddam was flouting Security Council resolutions?" Traub, *The Best of Intentions*, 186–87.

40. Shashi Tharoor, "Why America Still Needs the United Nations," *Foreign Affairs* (September/October 2003): 73.

41. P. Parameswaran, "Japan's Position on Myanmar Irks US," Agence France Presse online, June 4, 2006.

42. "Chávez: Bush 'Devil'; U.S. 'on the Way Down'," CNN.com online, September 21, 2006.

43. Warren Hoge, "Venezuelan's Diatribe Seen as Fatal to U.N. Council Bid," *New York Times*, October 25, 2006, A6.

44. Anne-Marie Slaughter, "Mercy Killings," *Foreign Policy* (May/June 2003): 72.

45. Even in 1990, legal scholar William O'Brien wrote: "Given that much of contemporary conflict takes the form of subversive intervention, exported revolution, indirect aggression and transnational revolutionary warfare emphasizing terrorism, strict interpretations of the right of self-defense against immediate

armed attacks are not compelling." Quoted in Anthony Clark Arend and Robert J. Beck, *International Law and the Use of Force* (London: Routledge, 1993), 160.

46. Glennon, *Limits of Law,* 167.

47. Marc Trachtenberg, "Intervention in Historical Perspective," in Laura W. Reed and Carl Kaysen, eds., *Emerging Norms of Justified Intervention* (Cambridge, Mass.: American Academy of Arts and Sciences, 1993), 30.

48. Michael Doyle, "Three Pillars of the Liberal Peace," *American Political Science Review* 99 (3) (August 2005): 464.

49. See Immanuel Kant, "Perpetual Peace," in *Kant: Political Writings,* ed. H. S. Reiss (Cambridge: Cambridge University Press, 2004), 93–130.

50. Glennon, *Limits of Law,* 151.

51. Kennedy, *Parliament of Man,* 253.

52. Brecher, "In Defence of Preventive War," 259.

53. Townsend Hoopes and Douglas Brinkley, *FDR and the Creation of the U.N.* (New Haven, Conn.: Yale University Press, 1997), 116.

54. Scholar James Sutterlin has argued for keeping the absolute veto, but limiting its use only to issues under Chapter VII or anything involving military force. Since these are the questions on which preventive action would deadlock, it is not clear how Sutterlin's proposal solves the problem, but it is a least an argument for limiting the veto. James Sutterlin, "The Past as Prologue," in Russett, ed., *The Once and Future Security Council,* 7.

55. Tharoor, "Why America Still Needs the United Nations," 50.

56. The American electoral college works in a similar way, requiring the smaller states and their votes in order to give a candidate enough votes to win the presidency. By design, it is almost impossible for an American president to win by grabbing the votes of only the largest states.

57. Interview with Gilles Andréani, Paris, October 19, 2006.

58. John M. Owen IV, "International Law and the 'Liberal Peace,'" in Gregory H. Fox and Brad R. Roth, eds., *Democratic Governance and International Law* (Cambridge: Cambridge University Press, 2000), 382–83.

59. George P. Schultz, "An Essential War," *The Wall St. Journal,* March 29, 2004, A18.

60. Kennedy, *Parliament of Man,* 263.

61. Glennon, *Limits of Law,* 177–78.

Afterword: Now What?

1. See Arnold Wolfers, *Discord and Collaboration: Essays on International Politics* (Baltimore: Johns Hopkins University Press, 1963), chap. 1.

2. Henry Kissinger, "The Rules on Preventive Force," *Washington Post,* April 9, 2006, B7.

Index